Robert Winston

P9-DFQ-773

WHAT MAKES ME ME?

Purchased from
Multnomah County Library
Title Wave Used Bookstore
216 NE Knott St, Portland, OR
503-988-5021

Senior editor Ben Morgan
Senior art editor Claire Patané
Category publisher Mary Ling
Art director Jane Bull
Publishing manager Sue Leonard
Managing art editor Clare Shedden
Editors Elizabeth Haldane, Zahavit Shalev, Susan Watt

REVISED EDITION
Senior editors Fleur Star, Bharti Bedi
Senior art editor Spencer Holbrook
Assistant editors Tejaswita Payal, Sheryl Sadana
Assistant art editor Nidhi Rastogi
DTP designer Sachin Gupta
Senior DTP designer Harish Aggarwal
Jacket designer Suhita Dharamjit
Jackets assistant Claire Gell
Jacket design development manager Sophia MTT
Producer, pre-production Gillian Reid
Producer Vivienne Yong
Managing editors Linda Esposito, Kingshuk Ghoshal
Managing art editors Philip Letsu, Govind Mittal
Publisher Andrew Macintyre
Publishing director Jonathan Metcalf
Associate publishing director Liz Wheeler
Design director Stuart Jackman

First American Edition, 2004
This edition published in the United States in 2015 by
DK Publishing, 345 Hudson Street, New York, New York 10014

Foreword copyright © 2004 Robert Winston
Copyright © 2004, 2015 Dorling Kindersley Limited
A Penguin Random House Company
15 16 17 18 19 10 9 8 7 6 5 4 3 2 1
001–283256–September/2015

All rights reserved.
Without limiting the rights under the copyright reserved above, no part of this publication
may be reproduced, stored in or introduced into a retrieval system, or transmitted, in any
form, or by any means (electronic, mechanical, photocopying, recording, or otherwise),
without the prior written permission of the copyright owner.
Published in Great Britain by Dorling Kindersley Limited.

A catalog record for this book is available from the Library of Congress.
ISBN 978-1-4654-3905-5 (Paperback)

DK books are available at special discounts when purchased
in bulk for sales promotions, premiums, fund-raising, or educational
use. For details, contact: DK Publishing Special Markets,
345 Hudson Street, New York, New York 10014
SpecialSales@dk.com

Printed and bound in China

A WORLD OF IDEAS:
SEE ALL THERE IS TO KNOW
www.dk.com

"Have you ever wondered why you hate Brussels sprouts so much, why your face is different from everybody else's, or why you sometimes sound exactly like your parents? Your body, your brain, and the way you think, act, and behave are all related—and they all contribute to making you different from everybody else.

This book is all about the things that make you individually you, from the shape of your ears and the sound of your voice to the things that really scare you or make you laugh. Your genes, your personality, and your talents are all part of the story, and you can find out more about them by taking the quizzes and tests in this book. Most of all, this book is designed to make it fun to find out just what makes you *you*. "

Robert Winston.

 What am **I MADE OF?**

 What makes me **UNIQUE?**

 How does my **BRAIN WORK?**

 What kind of **PERSON** am I?

 **TEST** yourself

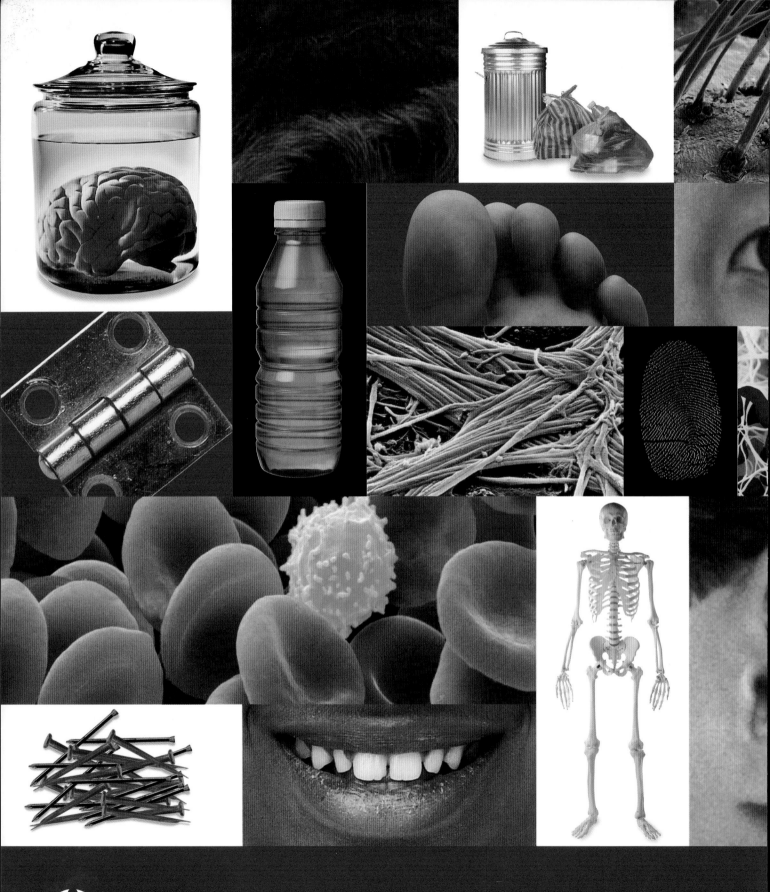

WHAT AM I MADE OF?

"Your body is a fantastically complicated machine made of 5 billion billion billion atoms.

People have been trying to figure out how the body works for at least 4,000 years, and there are still lots of mysteries—like how our brains work and why we hiccup.

But one thing we know for sure is what we're made of: just water, carbon, and a handful of simple chemical elements that you can find anywhere. In fact, you could dig up all the atoms you need to make a human body in your back yard garden."

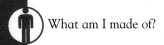

The INGREDIENTS

Imagine trying to build a human body from scratch, using the simplest ingredients possible. You could do it with only 13 chemicals, called **elements**. There's nothing special about the elements in the human body. We're made from exactly the same stuff as all other living things, from **fleas** to **whales**.

PHOSPHORUS

IRON

H_2O

CHLORINE

NITROGEN

CALCIUM

SULFUR

POTASSIUM

ONE HUMAN BODY

33 kg oxygen + 9kg carbon + 5kg
800g calcium + 500g phosphorus
sulfur + 80g sodium + 80g
+ 4g iron + 0.02g iodine

1 65% Oxygen
The element oxygen makes up about two-thirds of your body, mostly in the form of water (H_2O). You also take in oxygen from the air each time you breathe in.

2 18% Carbon
Nearly a fifth of you is carbon—the same element that coal, diamond, and the lead of pencils are made from. Carbon atoms link together in long chains, forming the backbone of all the most complex molecules inside you.

3 10% Hydrogen
Hydrogen is the most common element in the universe and also has the tiniest atoms. Hydrogen gas can **pass through walls** and float on air, which is why people used to fill balloons with it (until they discovered how easily it explodes).

4 3% Nitrogen
A bag of plant fertilizer contains about as much nitrogen as an average human body. Nitrogen is one of the main ingredients in your muscles. It's also the main ingredient in air.

5 1% Phosphorus
This element is what makes the tips of matches burst into flame. It also makes your teeth and bones strong, forms cell membranes, and helps carry energy.

SODIUM

IODINE

MAGNESIUM

CARBON

BEING COOKED UP...

hydrogen + 1.5kg nitrogen + + 180g potassium + 130g chlorine + 25g magnesium = **YOU!**

Is there anything else?

For a perfect body you also need a tiny bit of copper, zinc, manganese, cobalt, lithium, strontium, aluminum, silicon, lead, and arsenic. The average body also contains about 90 micrograms of **uranium**.

6 0.35% **Potassium**
Luxury soaps are made with potassium. Potassium also keeps your body fluids chemically balanced.

7 0.15% **Chlorine**
Chlorine is a **deadly green gas**, used to make bleach. In the body, it binds to sodium to form salt (sodium chloride).

8 0.15% **Sodium**
Sodium is the other half of sodium chloride (salt). Salt makes all your body fluids exactly as salty as seawater.

9 0.05% **Magnesium**
The dazzling white light of fireworks comes from burning magnesium. In your body, magnesium bolsters your immune system and helps nerves to fire and muscles to contract.

10 0.25% **Sulfur**
Sulfur is a vital part of proteins and helps your blood to clot. It is also responsible for the foul smell of farts, rotten eggs, and stagnant ponds.

11 1.6% **Calcium**
Calcium is what makes seashells, chalk, and marble hard. It does the same job in your bones and teeth, and it also keeps your heart beating and your muscles working.

12 0.008% **Iron**
There's just enough iron in your blood to make a nail. Iron turns red when it binds to oxygen, which is why blood and rust are red.

13 0.00004% **Iodine**
There's barely a pinch of iodine in your body, yet you'd die without it. Give iodine to tadpoles and they turn into frogs.

CELLS

You'd never build a human body simply by mixing chemical elements—that would be like expecting a storm in a junkyard to put together a jumbo jet. Instead, you need to start with the right building blocks. The tiniest building blocks are microscopic units called **cells**, but you'd need to collect up to **100 trillion** of these and arrange them in an impossibly complicated jigsaw puzzle. Here are just a few.

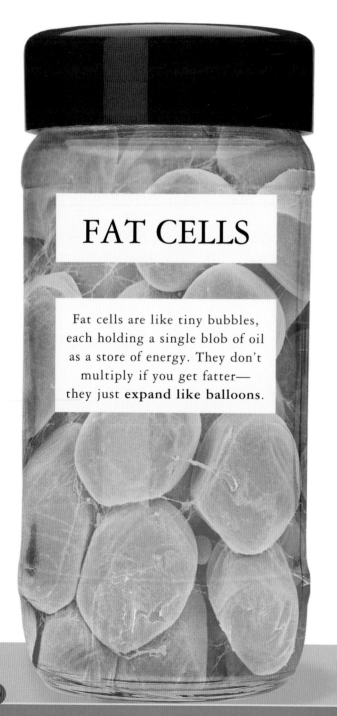

FAT CELLS

Fat cells are like tiny bubbles, each holding a single blob of oil as a store of energy. They don't multiply if you get fatter— they just **expand like balloons.**

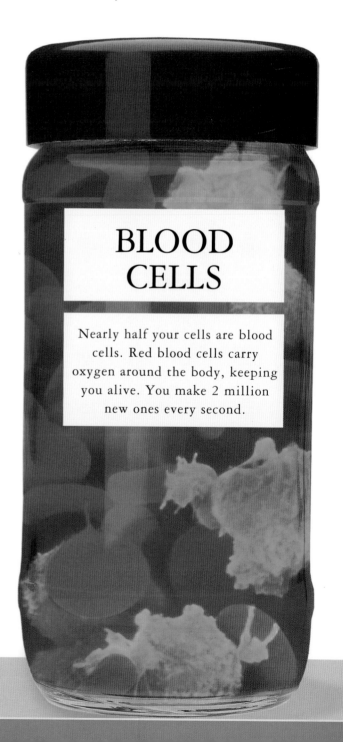

BLOOD CELLS

Nearly half your cells are blood cells. Red blood cells carry oxygen around the body, keeping you alive. You make 2 million new ones every second.

Eye cells
The cells in the back of your eyes detect light and so give you the sense of vision.

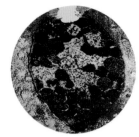

Goblet cell
The slimy liquid (**mucus**) in your nose and intestines comes from goblet cells.

Sperm cells
When a sperm cell from a man joins a woman's egg cell, they form a new baby.

Skin cells
Flaky skin cells protect your fragile insides from the world outside.

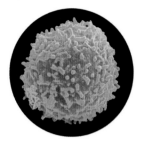

White blood cell
This cell is a kind of roving soldier. It searches for germs and **kills them.**

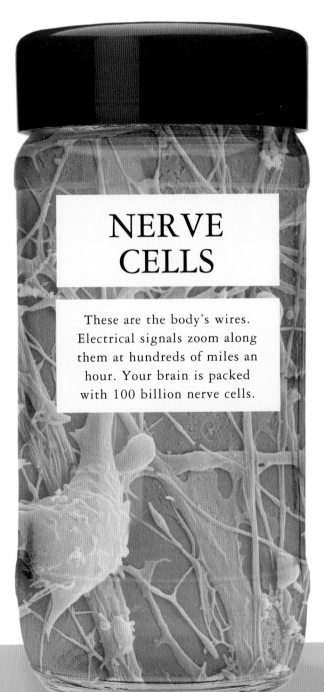

NERVE CELLS

These are the body's wires. Electrical signals zoom along them at hundreds of miles an hour. Your brain is packed with 100 billion nerve cells.

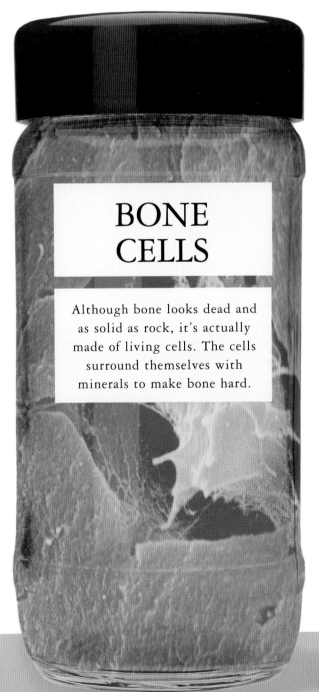

BONE CELLS

Although bone looks dead and as solid as rock, it's actually made of living cells. The cells surround themselves with minerals to make bone hard.

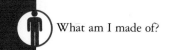

BODY PARTS

It would take **forever** to build a body from 100 trillion separate cells, but you could speed things up by starting with larger building blocks. Cells normally group together with cells of a similar type to make **tissues**, such as fat, nerves,

9 bottles of **blood**, 2 square yards (2 square meters) of **skin**, 5 million **hairs**, 1 bucket

Blood
Skin
Hair
Fat

Blood is a liquid tissue that carries vital supplies around the body. It's made of trillions of red cells suspended in a watery mix of salt, sugar, and other chemicals.

The largest organ is the skin, which protects the insides from damage. Its outer surface is continually wearing away.

Hairs cover the body except for the eyes, lips, palms, and soles of the feet.

The body stores spare energy as fat under the skin and around organs.

1 **heart**, 2 **lungs**, 2 **kidneys** plumbed into 1 **bladder**, 1 **stomach**, 9 yards (9 meters)

Lungs
Kidneys
Bladder
Stomach

Lungs suck in life-giving **oxygen** from the air and pass it to the blood.

The body is continually making waste chemicals. The kidneys filter out the waste and turn it into urine.

Urine from the kidneys drains into a stretchy bag called the bladder. When it fills up, it triggers the urge to urinate.

The stomach is a J-shaped chamber that churns food around and begins to break it down with acid.

or muscle. When two or more different tissues join together to make a body part with a specific job—such as the heart, stomach, or brain—we call it an **organ**. So what tissues and organs would you need to build a body?

of **fat**, 206 **bones** tied to 640 **muscles**, 62,000 miles (100,000 km) of **blood vessels**,

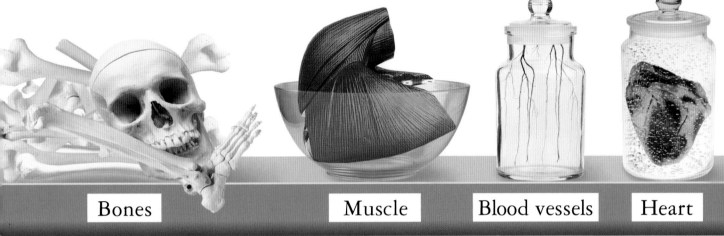

Bones

Bones make up the skeleton, which holds everything in place and makes movement possible, thanks to its amazingly flexible joints.

Muscle

Muscles pull on bones and move the body. Muscles also make up the walls of inner organs like the heart.

Blood vessels

Blood flows through tubes called blood vessels (arteries, veins, and capillaries).

Heart

This is the pump that drives blood around the body. It never stops (until you die).

of **intestines**, 1 **liver**, 32 **teeth**, 1 **brain**, and a set of **sense organs**.

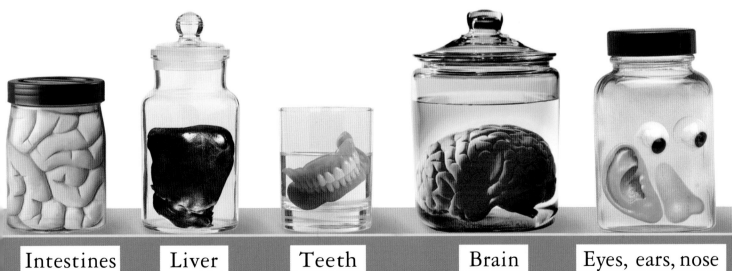

Intestines

These tangled tubes digest food into simple chemicals that the blood can absorb.

Liver

The liver is kind of chemical factory that processes chemicals in the blood.

Teeth

Teeth chop up food and mash it into a paste that is easy to swallow.

Brain

This is the body's control center and the smartest part, where thoughts, memories, and feelings happen.

Eyes, ears, nose

The eyes, ears, and nose are the most important sense organs.

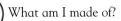

YOU

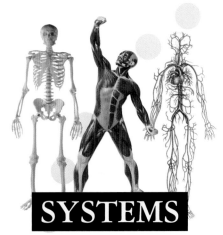

SYSTEMS

ELEMENTS

PUTTING EVERYTHING TOGETHER

ORGANS

CELLS

Once you've amassed a full set of **body parts**, you can start putting them together. Just as elements make cells and cells make organs, organs fit together in **systems**, each doing a particular job. The first system to build is the skeleton, which creates a frame for everything else. Then you simply add all the other organs, connect them together, wrap the whole works in a layer of skin, and switch on the sense organs.

SKELETON

The skeleton is an inner framework of bones that holds the body in place. Without a skeleton, you'd collapse on the floor like jelly. About 25 percent of your body weight is bone, and half your 206 bones are in your hands and feet. The bones are held together by an ingenious system of **joints** and hinges that let the whole body move.

Bones feel pain and bleed when cut

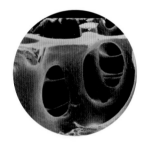

What's in a bone?

Bones aren't as solid and heavy as they look. Their insides are riddled with **hollow spaces** to keep them light and to carry blood vessels and nerves.

How do they heal?

Bone is a **living tissue**—it can grow or heal itself just as skin can. When you break a bone, new bone tissue quickly forms and plugs the gap. If you exercise, your bones get denser and stronger.

What are joints?

Joints lock bones together but also allow them to move to some extent. The joints in your fingers, elbows, and knees work like **hinges**, restricting movement mostly to one direction only.

How do hips work?

Hips and shoulders are **ball-and-socket** joints. This clever design lets your arms and legs swing freely in any direction. As with all mobile joints, a capsule of fluid surrounds the joint and keeps it working smoothly.

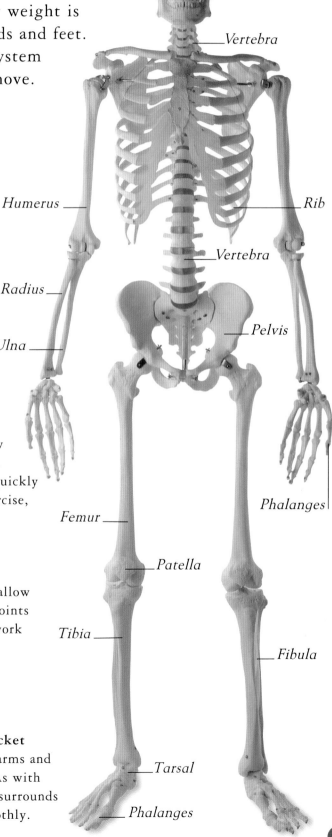

Skull

Vertebra

Humerus

Rib

Vertebra

Radius

Pelvis

Ulna

Phalanges

Femur

Patella

Tibia

Fibula

Tarsal

Phalanges

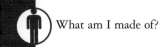

MUSCLES

Muscles are what make you move. Your biggest muscles wrap around bones and are tied in place with tough, stringy cords called **tendons**. When muscles contract, they pull on the bones and move your skeleton. You have conscious control of about 640 muscles, but there are hundreds more that you can't move voluntarily.

About 40% of your body weight is muscle

Fake smile
The **60 muscles** in your face are only partly voluntary. A fake smile uses a different set of muscles from those in a genuine, involuntary smile.

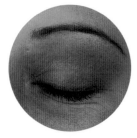

Blinking fast
Your fastest muscles are in your eyelids. They make you blink about 20 times a minute to keep your eyes moist. If you didn't blink, your eyes would dry out and you'd **go blind**.

My finger's stuck!
Put your hand in this position and lift each finger one by one. Your ring finger is stuck because it's tied to the same tendon as the middle finger.

Tongue-twister
The most flexible part of your body is your tongue. It is made of at least **14 muscles** wrapped in a complicated bundle that can twist and turn in any direction.

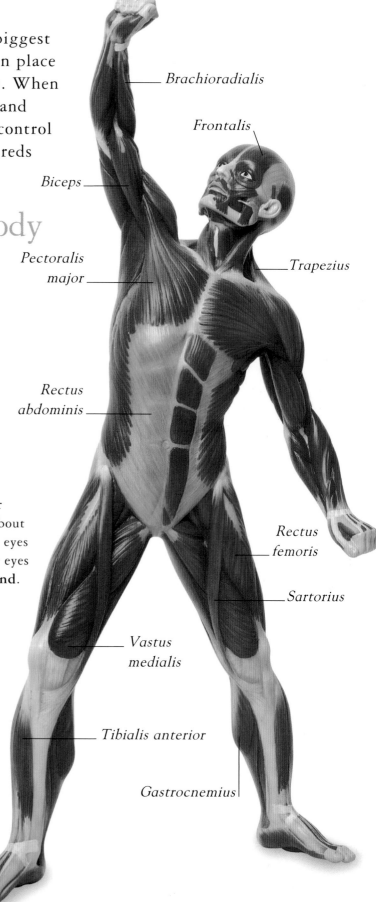

Brachioradialis

Frontalis

Biceps

Pectoralis major

Trapezius

Rectus abdominis

Rectus femoris

Sartorius

Vastus medialis

Tibialis anterior

Gastrocnemius

CIRCULATORY SYSTEM

Blood is the body's transportation system. Pumped by the heart, it shoots around the body through tubes called blood vessels, delivering all the **oxygen**, food, and chemicals that cells need. It also carries cells to fight germs, and it takes away waste materials and spreads heat. You can lose about a third of your blood and still survive, but if you lose half, you die.

Your heart beats about 100,000 times a day

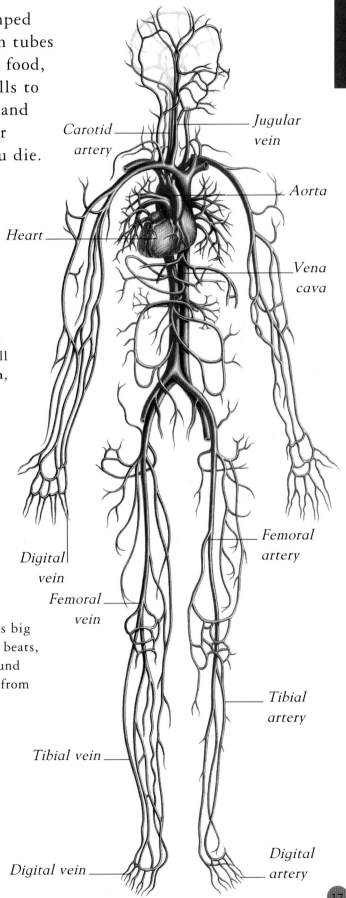

Carotid artery

Jugular vein

Aorta

Heart

Vena cava

Femoral artery

Digital vein

Femoral vein

Tibial artery

Tibial vein

Digital vein

Digital artery

Red blood cells

A single drop of blood contains about 5 million red blood cells. They are full of the iron-rich chemical **hemoglobin**, which picks up oxygen in the lungs and then releases it around the body.

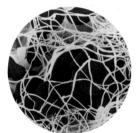

Blood clot

When you cut yourself, chemicals in the blood react with air and form a tangle of sticky fibers that trap blood cells like fish in a net. The clot dries to become a scab.

Heart

The heart is a hollow ball of muscle as big as a fist, but much stronger. When it beats, it squirts about a cupful of blood around your body. **Arteries** take blood away from the heart and **veins** bring it back.

Check your pulse

Your pulse is blood stopping and starting with each beat of your heart. Your heart normally beats about 70 times a minute, but it can go up to 200 if you're excited.

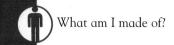
NERVOUS SYSTEM

This system allows your body to react to the world with **lightning speed**. It works like a network of electric wires and cables, but it carries information instead of power. Its control center is the brain, which takes in signals from the sense organs, processes the information, and sends out new **signals** that tell the body how to react.

Signals zoom along nerves at 250 mph (400 kph)

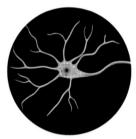

What's a neuron?
The nervous system is made of cells called neurons, which have spindly fibers that carry electrical signals. Some neurons have fibers several feet long.

Nerve
Nerves are the body's major cables and contain hundreds of neuron fibers. The fibers run to every nook and cranny of the body.

Bridging the gap
When an electrical signal reaches the end of a neuron, a tiny gap called a **synapse** stops it from jumping to the next cell. Chemicals called neurotransmitters cross the gap and trigger the next cell, passing the signal on.

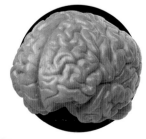

Control center
Your brain is about the size of a coconut and has a wrinkled surface like a walnut. It connects to the rest of the nervous system via a tube of neurons called the **spinal cord**.

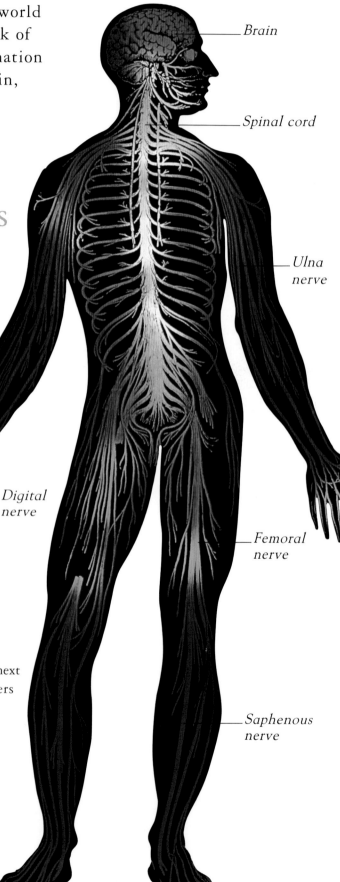

Brain

Spinal cord

Ulna nerve

Digital nerve

Femoral nerve

Saphenous nerve

DIGESTIVE SYSTEM

Everything you eat passes through your digestive system—a long, complicated tube that runs through your body and takes up most of the space in your belly. The digestive organs produce powerful chemicals called **enzymes**. These attack the large molecules in food and break them into tiny fragments that your body can **absorb**.

A meal takes 18–30 hours to pass through you

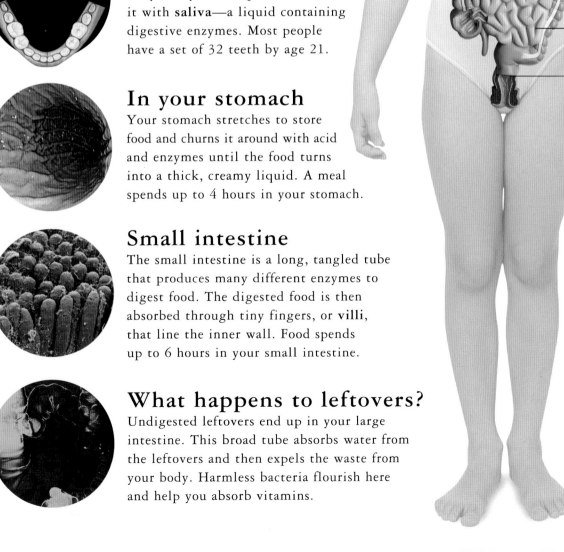

Salivary gland

Esophagus

Liver

Stomach

Large intestine

Small intestine

Rectum

Teeth

These are the hardest parts of your body. They break up food and mix it with **saliva**—a liquid containing digestive enzymes. Most people have a set of 32 teeth by age 21.

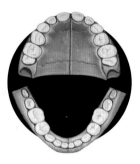

In your stomach

Your stomach stretches to store food and churns it around with acid and enzymes until the food turns into a thick, creamy liquid. A meal spends up to 4 hours in your stomach.

Small intestine

The small intestine is a long, tangled tube that produces many different enzymes to digest food. The digested food is then absorbed through tiny fingers, or **villi**, that line the inner wall. Food spends up to 6 hours in your small intestine.

What happens to leftovers?

Undigested leftovers end up in your large intestine. This broad tube absorbs water from the leftovers and then expels the waste from your body. Harmless bacteria flourish here and help you absorb vitamins.

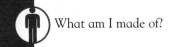
RESPIRATORY SYSTEM

All your body's cells need a supply of the life-giving gas **oxygen**, which comes from the air. Your respiratory system takes in oxygen and passes it to your blood. The main organs in this system are your **lungs**, which suck in air whenever you breathe. They work like giant sponges, except that they take in air instead of water.

You breathe in and out 23,000 times a day

Voice box

Windpipe

Lung

Heart

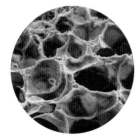

In and out

Air travels to your lungs through a tube in your neck called the windpipe, or **trachea**. The windpipe splits into smaller and smaller branches, forming a maze of airways throughout the lungs.

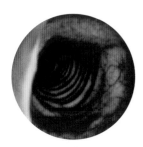

Air pockets

The airways end in tiny pockets called **alveoli**. Blood flows around these, picking up oxygen and getting rid of the waste gas carbon dioxide. Your lungs have about 600 million alveoli—if you laid them out flat, they'd cover a tennis court.

Keeping clean

Air contains dirt and germs, which your lungs must get rid of. Coughing and sneezing help clear the worst of it. Your airways also secrete a layer of sticky **mucus** to trap dirt. The mucus is carried up to the back of your throat and swallowed.

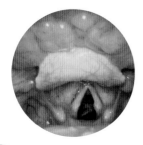

Making noise

Your voice comes from a chamber called the voice box at the top of your windpipe. As you breathe out, air passes between two small flaps of tissue. When these are drawn together, they **vibrate** and create sound. The tighter they are, the higher the pitch.

SKIN AND HAIR

About 22 square feet (2 square meters) of skin protects your body from dirt, germs, cold, and injury. This tough, waterproof layer is your biggest sense organ—it's packed with nerves that sense touch, pain, and heat. Your skin's outermost layer is continually wearing away, so it **replaces itself completely** about once a month.

The entire surface of your body is dead

Get a grip

The swirling ridges of skin on the tips of your fingers are there to help you grip things. Along the ridges are tiny pores that secrete sweat and oil to improve your grip.

Shed your skin

The surface of your skin consists of tough, dried-out flakes of dead tissue. These are continually rubbing off—you shed about **10 billion** a day. Most of the dust in your home is old skin flakes.

Hair today

Thick hair covers the top of your head to keep your brain warm, and the rest of your body is covered by fine hairs. (You have as many hairs as a chimpanzee.) Each hair has a **tiny muscle** that can make it stand up when you're cold.

Sweat and smells

You make at least half a pint of sweat a day. Your skin produces two types of sweat: eccrine sweat, which cools you down; and apocrine sweat, which gives you **B.O.** Your apocrine sweat glands become more active when you reach your teens.

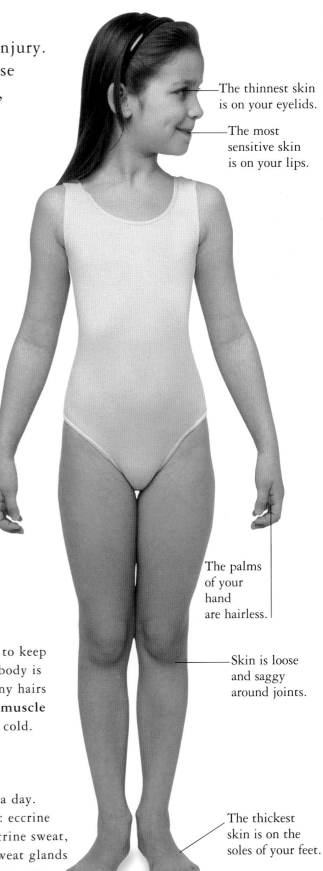

The thinnest skin is on your eyelids.

The most sensitive skin is on your lips.

The palms of your hand are hairless.

Skin is loose and saggy around joints.

The thickest skin is on the soles of your feet.

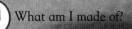

VISION

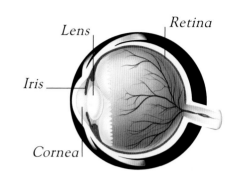

Lens Retina

Iris

Cornea

HEARING

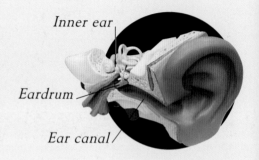

Inner ear

Eardrum

Ear canal

SMELL

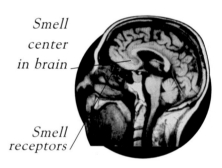

Smell center in brain

Smell receptors

TASTE

Bitter

Sour Sour

Salty Salty

Sweet

TOUCH

The five senses

VISION is our top sense. We can see more colors and better detail than most animals can, but our vision is terrible in darkness. Each eye is a 1-inch-wide (2.5-cm-wide) ball of transparent **jelly** that works like a camera. Light enters a hole called the pupil and is focused by a lens onto the **retina**—a sheet of light-sensitive cells in the back of the eye. These cells detect the color and strength of the light and send signals to the brain, which builds an image.

HEARING is the ability to sense invisible **vibrations** in air—sound. The odd shape of the outer ears funnels sound and helps tell where it comes from. The sound passes along a thin canal to the middle ear, where a miniature drum and a set of tiny levers transmit the vibrations from the air to liquid in the inner ear. Nerve cells in the inner ear then send signals to the brain.

SMELL is the ability to sense odor molecules floating in air. This sense is more important than you might think. The flavor of food actually depends more on smell than taste. The average person can recognize 4,000 different smells, and a well-trained nose can recognize 10,000. The smell molecules are detected by a patch of neurons high up in each nostril. When an odor molecule binds to a matching neuron, it triggers a signal.

TASTE is your ability to detect simple chemicals inside your mouth. When you chew food, these chemicals dissolve in your saliva and trigger taste buds, mainly on your tongue. The best-known tastes are sweet, salty, bitter, and sour, which are located on different parts of the tongue. Taste buds can also detect a chemical called **glutamate**, which makes food taste meaty and savory.

TOUCH receptors cover your entire body. Different types of receptors sense different types of touch, such as light pressure, heavy pressure, hair movements, and vibration. Touch is all about movement—we **actively explore** objects with our fingers, lips, and tongue. With touch alone, we can identify even the different coins in a pocket without looking at them.

DO I HAVE A SIXTH SENSE?

The human body has far more than five senses. Here are just a few of the things your special senses can detect:

Gravity

Deep in your inner ear are tiny gravity sensors called **otoliths**. These tell your brain which way is up or down, helping you balance.

Motion

Your inner ear also contains motion sensors that can sense movement in any direction. If you spin around and around, they stop working and make you dizzy.

Heat

Heat sensors all over your skin can feel warmth or cold, even at a distance. Your lips and tongue are the most heat-sensitive parts of your body. They can tell whether a drink is too hot without touching it.

Pain

Pain is a special sense triggered by damage to your body. Pain has a purpose because it makes you leave the damaged area alone. Itching and tickling are both a mixture of touch and pain.

Muscles

Your muscles contain **stretch sensors** that tell your brain what each part of your body is doing. This makes you aware of the whole body. Without it, you wouldn't be able to stand still, move around, or pick things up.

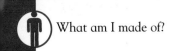
Are you allergic to...?

GRASS POLLEN	HOUSEHOLD DUST	DUSTMITE FAECES	CAT HAIR	PEANUTS	WHEAT PROTEIN	COCKROACH DUNG

FAQ

Why do I cough and sneeze?

If germs get through your nose or mouth, your body will try to get rid of them. Coughs and sneezes blow germs out of your lungs and airways. Vomiting and diarrhea get rid of germs that have gotten into your stomach or intestines.

Why do cuts swell up?

If germs get under your skin, white blood cells soon find them. They release the chemical histamine, which makes blood rush to the area. The blood-filled zone becomes **inflamed**—red, swollen, hot, and unusually sensitive to pain. Inflamed skin is not necessarily damaged—it just means your immune system is doing its job.

What do antibodies do?

Antibodies are molecules that identify and stick to germs. There are millions of differently shaped antibodies floating around in your body fluids. When one meets a germ whose surface molecules match its shape, it locks onto it and tells your white blood cells to **attack** the germ.

Immune SYSTEM

Every time you sneeze, cough, vomit, or get a scratch, a bite, a cut, a swelling, a rash, a zit, a cold, an upset stomach, a runny nose, diarrhea, or a raging temperature, you are seeing your **immune system** at work.

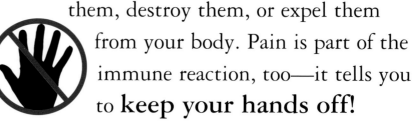

Your immune system never stops hunting for **germs** and doing everything it can to isolate them, destroy them, or expel them from your body. Pain is part of the immune reaction, too—it tells you to **keep your hands off!**

| INSECT STINGS | MOULD SPORES | SHELLFISH | POISON IVY | PENICILLIN | LATEX | LAUNDRY DETERGENT |

Why am I allergic?

Your immune system has to deal with thousands of different invaders, from viruses to flesh-eating maggots. With such a tough job to do, it's bound to **make mistakes**. Sometimes it attacks harmless substances (allergens) as though they were germs, and this is what causes **allergies** and **asthma**. You're more likely to develop allergies if you grow up in a very clean home, where your immune system does not get much practice attacking real germs.

The symptoms of an allergy depend on where the allergen makes contact with your body.

AIRWAYS

Sneezing, coughing, and breathing difficulties can happen when you breathe in allergens like dust or pollen.

DIGESTIVE TRACT

If you swallow allergens, your digestive system reacts as though germs have gotten into it and tries to expel the food. This may cause stomach cramps, vomiting, or diarrhea.

MOUTH

Food allergies can make your mouth tingle and your lips and tongue swell up.

SKIN

A rash or blisters may break out on your skin if you touch something that causes an allergy. Some allergic rashes are just like the itchy lumps produced by stinging nettles.

FAQ

Why don't I self-destruct?

Your immune system would attack your own cells if they did not have a kind of molecular name tag. The tag is made up of a set of proteins called the major histocompatibility complex (MHC), and it's **utterly unique** to you.

What's sex got to do with it?

Germs breed very quickly and keep changing. Some of the new forms manage to sneak past the human immune system by mimicking our MHC proteins. One of the reasons we reproduce sexually is to outsmart these germs. Sexual reproduction gives everyone different MHC proteins, scrambling the cellular combination locks that protect us.

Can you smell true love?

Some scientists think that we instinctively choose partners who will give our children varied MHC proteins—and hence a strong immune system. We seem to do this by **smell**. Overall, people tend to prefer the body odor of a partner whose MHC genes are very different from their own.

WHAT MAKES ME UNIQUE?

> " Though we're all built to the same plan,
> we're also completely different from each other.
> There are hundreds of things that make you
> different from everyone else, from your taste in
> music and your sense of humor to the sound of
> your voice and the shape of your face.

So how did you become unique?

> Part of the answer lies in your genes.
> Your parents would have to have another
>
> # 1,000,000,000,000,000
>
> babies to stand a chance of having another
> child with the same genes as you. And part of
> the answer lies in the experiences that shape
> your personality as you grow up. "

UNIQUE TO YOU

Imagine someone stole your I.D., had plastic surgery to look just like you, and then **pretended to be you**. Could they get away with it? Fortunately, there are lots of ways of proving you're the real you, and

FINGERPRINTS IRIS IMMUNE SYSTEM

WHORL   COMPOSITE

Core   *Ridge dot*

ARCH   LOOP

Lake   *Delta*

The patterns on your fingertips are utterly unique. Even **identical twins** have different fingerprints, though their footprints and handprints are very similar. Fingerprints stay the same for life, and if you injure the skin, the same prints grow back. Your left and right prints might look like mirror images, but if you look carefully, you'll see they're all unique.

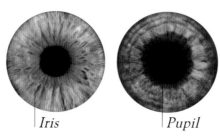

Iris   *Pupil*

The colored part of your eye is your iris, and it's as unique as a fingerprint. Each iris has a complicated pattern of stripes and gaps that an iris scanner can read to make a pattern like a bar code (below). Iris scans aren't perfect, though. Your irises change when you're ill, and you can hide your identity by wearing contact lenses.

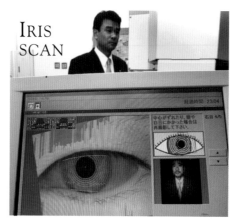

IRIS SCAN

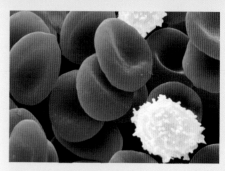

Your white blood cells can tell your cells apart from those of other people.

Your immune system can distinguish your cells from all others. If foreign cells (such as germs) get into your body, your white blood cells spot them and attack. Unfortunately, this system works so well that your body will try to **reject** organs transplanted from another person, even if you'd die without them. Organ transplants work best between close relatives, and best of all between identical twins, whose immune systems can't tell the difference between them.

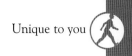

How would you prove you're the real *you*?

they're all based on the fact that everyone is **biologically unique**. Some of these tests are so effective that police can use them to catch criminals from the tiny clues left at the scene of a crime.

DNA   VOICE   SIGNATURE

A very good way of proving who you are is to get a **DNA fingerprint**. This is made by breaking a sample of your DNA into fragments and then letting these spread through a sheet of gel to make a pattern of bands. Police use DNA fingerprints to work out the identity of people from blood, hair, or other body tissues found at the scene of a crime. According to some experts, the chance of two people having the same DNA fingerprint is 1 in 5,000 billion billion.

"B A B Y"

Although your voice changes with your mood, with your choice of words, and with your age, there are certain tones that **stay distinctive** for life. A voiceprint analyzer can extract and recognize these sounds, even if you're talking on the phone. Some large banks use voiceprints to check the identity of their staff.

Everyone has distinctive **handwriting**, and people called graphologists claim to be able to tell what kind of personality someone has from their handwriting. The traditional way of proving your identity is to write a signature. This is written in one quick action, exaggerating your style of handwriting in a way that makes the signature harder to fake. But signatures are not a foolproof way of proving your identity because they are usually judged by eye.

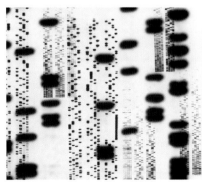

DNA banding patterns like this can be used to find out who your relatives are or to make unique DNA fingerprints.

Voiceprint analyzers turn a person's voice into a pattern of lines on a computer.

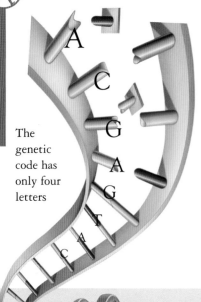

The genetic code has only four letters

What is a GENE?

The word gene has several meanings, but in essence, a gene is an instruction that tells your body how to work. The instruction is stored as a code in the molecule DNA.

DNA
Deoxyribonucleic acid

CHROMOSOMES

Nucleus

CELLS

You share 99% of your genes with a chimp, 85% with a mouse, and 50% with a banana!

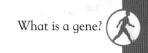

Gene can mean...

- a length of DNA • a code for making a protein
- an instruction that tells a cell what to do
- a controller that switches other genes on or off
- something you inherit from your parents—a unit of heredity

DNA CARRIES GENES. DNA is an amazingly long but ultra-thin molecule. It is shaped like a **twisted ladder**, the rungs of which make up a simple code with only four letters: A, C, G, and T (the letters stand for chemicals in the rungs). A gene is a segment of DNA containing a particular **sequence of letters**—a bit like a paragraph in a book. In most genes, the sequence of letters is a code for the sequence of different units (amino acids) in a protein molecule. Genes carry the code for many thousands of different proteins.

TCACCGTG
GTGGGCCTTGT
GGGTGCCTTCCGA
ATTCGAATTCCCTTG
TGGATGCCAATATAC
GCATATAGGCACAC
CGTGGTGGGCCT
TGTGGGTGCC
TTCCG

CHROMOSOMES CARRY DNA. Your DNA has to fit into a **tiny** space, so it is packed up in an ingenious way. Each molecule of DNA is coiled to make a thread, the thread is coiled again to make a cord, and so on (just as thin fibers can be wound together to make rope). The end result is a chunky, X-shaped structure called a **chromosome**. Chromosomes are far too small to see with the naked eye— you'd need about 100,000 of them just to fill a period. Even so, each chromosome contains a **whopping** 7 feet (2 meters) of DNA.

CELLS CARRY CHROMOSOMES. Each cell in your body (with a few exceptions) contains a set of 46 chromosomes squashed together inside the cell nucleus. The full set of 46 chromosomes carries **all your genes**, so you have a complete set of genes inside every cell. That's an **awful lot** of DNA! If you unraveled all the DNA from every chromosome in every cell in your body and laid the molecules end to end, your DNA would stretch to the Sun and back **400 times**. Yet all the information in your genes could be stored on a **single CD**.

ALL YOUR DNA = YOUR GENOME. The DNA in one set of chromosomes makes up your **genome**. There are only about 30,000 working genes in the human genome—the rest of the DNA is mostly **junk**. The human genome is very similar to that of many other species, even bananas! This is because all organisms share the same distant ancestors, and most of our genes are concerned with the nuts and bolts of making cells work. **Evolution** only has to tinker with a few genes to make a big difference in the way our bodies look and work.

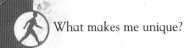

Where are my GENES from?

Your genes come from your parents, theirs come from their parents, and so on—all the way back to the first living thing that ever existed. Genes are passed down through families, and that's why you probably look a bit like your parents. Physical characteristics, like **long eyelashes, red hair, freckles,** or **blue eyes,** run in families because they are controlled by genes.

Half your genes come from your mother and half come from your father.

They were passed on to you in **chromosomes** carried by sperm and egg cells. Sperm and egg cells have only 23 chromosomes each—half the usual amount. When they meet and form an embryo, they create a new person with a full set of 46 chromosomes.

46 CHROMOSOMES
MOM

46 CHROMOSOMES
DAD

46 CHROMOSOMES
YOU

23 ARE PASSED ON TO YOU

ARE PASSED ON TO YOU 23

You actually have **two sets** of genes: one set from your mother and another from your father. These two **genomes** give you a mixture of your mother's and father's features—perhaps you have your mother's hair and your father's eyes, for instance.

Every child in a family is different because your parent's genes are **shuffled** and then divided in two before making each sperm and egg cell. So each child gets a unique set of genes (except for identical twins).

Your genome is a **mosaic** of genes from all your **grandparents**

What's a dominant gene?

Since you have two sets of genes, you have **two options** for everything. Take eye color, for instance. You get eye-color genes from both parents, but you might get a gene for brown eyes from your mother and one for blue eyes from your father. Sometimes one option takes priority over the other—we call it a dominant gene. The brown-eye gene is usually dominant over the blue-eye gene, for instance.

If one of your parents has blue eyes...

...and the other has brown eyes...

...you'll *probably* have brown eyes, too.

Genes that are overpowered by dominant genes are **recessive**. For a recessive gene to have an effect, you'll need two copies—one from each parent. **Stick your thumb up.** If you can bend the tip of the thumb back, you have a "hitchhiker's thumb," which is caused by two recessive genes, one from each parent. Characteristics like this often skip a generation, appearing in grandparents and grandchildren but not in the parents.

What makes me a boy or a girl?

Two of your 46 chromosomes are special—they control your sex. These **sex chromosomes** are shaped like the letters **X** and **Y**. If you have two Xs, you're a girl (usually). If you have an X and a Y, you're a boy. In boys, all the genes on the X-chromosome have an effect whether or not they are dominant, because there isn't a matching X to complement them. This makes boys especially prone to genetic defects like color-blindness.

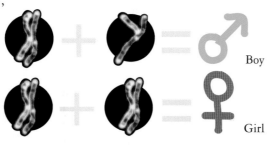

Boy

Girl

IS THERE A GENE FOR EVERYTHING?

Some genes have a very simple and obvious effect. A single gene can make you color-blind or give you red hair, for instance. So you might think there's a gene for each of your characteristics, from the shape of your face to the length of your legs. However, the truth is not so simple. Many, perhaps most, of your characteristics involve lots of genes working together. Your height, your looks, the texture of your skin, the sound of your voice, the color of your hair, and so on, probably all depend on the combination of genes you have.

Things get even more complicated when it comes to genes that affect your brain. Genes can certainly have an influence on how smart, outgoing, adventurous, or creative you are. But they don't **determine** your personality—they just **influence** how it might develop. And so do many other factors, such as your family, your friends, the decisions you make in life, and luck.

Why can't I stand milk?

If you hate milk, you aren't alone. Most of the world's people are **lactose-intolerant**, which means that milk gives them stomach pain, indigestion, and worse. The cause is a **recessive gene**. Most Asian and Afro-Caribbean people have this gene, but people from northwest Europe usually don't. Scientists think Europeans evolved a different gene when they started

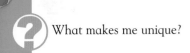
TEST YOUR GENES

1 TONGUE-ROLLING

Can you roll your tongue into a U-shape? (Don't cheat by squeezing your lips.)

2 BENT PINKIE

If the top part of your little finger bends toward the next finger, you have a "bent pinkie."

3 CONVEX NOSE

A nose that curves outward instead of inward is described as a convex or Roman nose.

5 CLEFT CHIN

A crease in the bottom of your chin is called a cleft chin. It's caused by a single dominant gene.

6 WIDOW'S PEAK

A widow's peak is a V-shaped pattern in your hairline, revealed when you brush your hair back.

7 FRECKLES

Freckles are spots of darker color on your skin. They are more pronounced when you're tanned.

9 DIMPLES

A dimple is a small dent that appears in one or both cheeks when you smile.

10 HITCHHIKER'S THUMB

If your thumb bends back more than 30°, you have a hitchhiker's thumb, which is caused by a recessive gene.

11 DARWIN'S EAR POINT
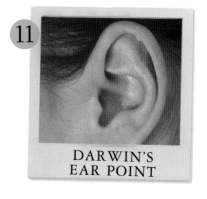

Feel the outer fold of your ear to see if you have a small point of skin called a Darwin's ear point.

Take the genes test. Most of these characteristics can be caused by a single dominant gene.

4

FREE EARLOBE

If your earlobe hangs free at the bottom, you have the dominant gene; otherwise, you have the recessive gene.

8

DIGITAL HAIR

If hair grows on the middle segment of your fingers or toes, you have the gene for "mid-digital hair."

12

HAND CLASPING

When you clasp your hands, which thumb is on top? The way that feels right is partly due to your genes.

WHAT DOES IT MEAN?

Blame your parents

All your genes come from your parents, so any characteristic caused by a dominant gene will probably also appear in one of your parents. If you can roll your tongue, the chances are that your mother or father can, too. And at least one of your four grandparents will have the dominant trait.

Be a DNA detective

With a bit of detective work, you can trace the path that genes take through your family by making a family tree. Collect photos of your relatives and glue them to a large piece of paper, with lines showing who is related to whom. Test everyone for the genes on this page and and write the results under the pictures.

Are you colour blind?

If you can't see a number in this circle of coloured dots, you might be colour blind. Colour blindness is caused by a **recessive gene** on the X-chromosome. Girls who inherit the gene usually have normal vision, but boys become colour blind. Test your family for colour blindness. If you or any of your brothers are colour blind, the gene almost certainly came from your mother.

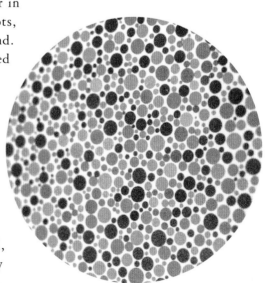

DOUBLE

How do twins form?

Identical twins form when, for unknown reasons, an embryo splits and develops as two separate babies. **Fraternal twins** are different. They form when two egg cells are fertilized by two sperm. Like ordinary brothers and sisters, they share only half their genes—they just happen to develop at the same time and share the womb.

Are **TWINS** really

Imagine what life would be like if there were two of you. That's a bit what being an identical twin is like. To scientists, identical twins are just like clones because they have the **same genes**. Because of this, twins give us a fascinating insight into how much genes can affect our personality.

Jim and Jim

Identical twins who grow up separately often turn out to be uncannily similar. Jim Springer first met his twin Jim Lewis in 1979 at age 40. They had identical voices and were both overweight with high blood pressure, bitten nails, haemorrhoids, and migraines. They went to the same beach for holidays and both had a dog called Toy. They were keen carpenters and both had built a white bench around a tree in the garden.

WHAT DO TWIN

Since identical twins have the same genes, any differences between them must be due to the environment in which they grow up (or chance). By studying the personality traits of lots of twins (especially twins who were adopted at birth and brought up in different families), scientists can actually measure how much of the variation in each trait is caused by genes. In other words, twin studies can help us begin to disentangle the effects of **nature** and **nurture**.

TROUBLE
DENTICAL?

How identical are you?

Some identical twins are more alike than others. Most identical twins share 100 percent of their genes, but a few rare twins might share only 75 percent. These **half-identical** twins are thought to form when an egg cell splits *before* being fertilized by two different sperm. If the egg cell splits just *after* being fertilized, normal identical twins develop, each with its own placenta. But if the embryo splits 4–5 days after the egg is fertilized, the twins share a placenta and may become **mirror twins**. If an embryo splits around two weeks after fertilization, the cells may not separate entirely, resulting in **conjoined twins**.

FAQ

What are mirror twins?

A quarter of identical twins are also mirror twins, which means that, in some respects, they look like mirror images of each other. Their fingerprints and the whorls in their hair look almost like reflections, and they may have the same pattern of moles or birthmarks, but on opposite sides of their bodies.

STUDIES TELL US?

THE RESULTS

Twin studies reveal that genes have a big influence on...

- what you look like
- your need to wear glasses
- your tendency to put on weight
- the medical problems you might have
- the main aspects of your personality (see p. 68)
- the fervor of your beliefs (but not what you believe)
- how long you might live
- your IQ

But genes have less influence on...

- whether you're right- or left-handed
- the food you like best
- your sense of humor

What are conjoined twins?

Conjoined twins are identical twins that don't completely separate and are born physically attached. Sometimes only a small patch of skin and muscle joins them, making it easy for doctors to separate them. In other cases, conjoined twins share vital internal organs such as the brain or spinal cord, which makes separating them very difficult and dangerous.

How did I DEVELOP?

Your genes control the amazing process of **development** that transforms you from a single cell into a body with 100 trillion cells. From the very beginning, your **environment** also plays a role in making you unique. And it continues to influence you for life as your brain keeps learning and changing.

> How did I begin?

> How fast did I grow?

> When did my eyes start to appear?

> When did my fingerprints form?

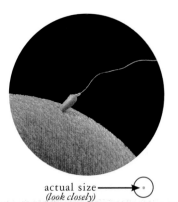

actual size ——▶
(look closely)

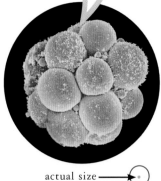

actual size ——▶

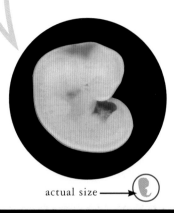

actual size ——▶

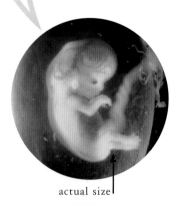

actual size

DAY 1

You spend the first half-hour of life as a single cell less than a tenth of a millimeter wide. This cell, called an **embryo**, forms when a sperm cell from your father fuses with an egg cell from your mother. The genes from your mother and father join together in the cell nucleus, giving you a unique genome.

3 DAYS

You don't grow much in the first few days. Instead, you divide. The single cell divides into 2, then 4, then 8, and so on, doubling in number each time. Within a week there are hundreds of cells, and over the next two weeks a body slowly begins to take shape. By three weeks, you have grown to the size of a **grain of rice**.

4 WEEKS

At 4 weeks, you look like a **shrimp** and have a tail. Your head is growing amazingly quickly and takes up nearly half your body. Arms are starting to form from buds, and dark spots mark the beginnings of your eyes. If your mother is undernourished at this stage, you are more likely to be overweight as an adult.

8 WEEKS

By 8 weeks, you are recognizably human but partly **transparent**. Your eyes, nose, lips, and even your teeth are forming, and your heart has started beating. By 12 weeks, you can move your arms and legs; your fingerprints have formed; you can swallow and urinate; and your brain is working.

When did I first suck my thumb?

When did I start to dream?

When did my eyes open?

When did I first hear?

When did I learn my mother's voice?

What could I do when I was born?

16 WEEKS

You are now about the size of a **lemon** and have become much more active. You can clench your fists, suck your thumb, make facial expressions, and grasp the umbilical cord that connects you to your mother. You start to **hear** your first sounds, but your eyes are not open yet.

20 WEEKS

Your activity level begins to show at this stage. You might kick a lot and do somersaults, for instance. If so, you'll probably be noisy and active after birth as well. You can hear well, and loud bangs will make you jump. Your sense of taste has developed, and you have a preference for sweet things. Your entire body is covered by **fine hair** that will disappear later.

24 WEEKS

Between 22 and 24 weeks, your eyes open. You can't see much, though, because it's dark in the womb, but you might see sunlight as a pink glow. Your hearing is now so good that you can recognize your **mother's voice**. When you sleep, you spend most of your time dreaming.

BIRTH

You can breathe, suck, and swallow from the moment you are born. You can cry, cough, sneeze, and blink, and your senses of smell and hearing are very good. Your vision, however, is poor. Although you can distinguish colors and see faces, you can see things clearly only if they are very close. And, of course, you don't yet know what anything is.

How did I learn
to speak?

When did
I start to
smile?

When did
I begin to
walk?

When did
my personality
start to show?

1ST 6 MONTHS

Your brain is already a quarter of adult size at birth, and it doubles in just 6 months. Your vision rapidly improves and is almost perfect by 6 months. You are fascinated by faces, and you can mirror your parents' **smiles** and frowns from birth. At 6 weeks old, you can stick out your tongue, at 5 months you recognize your name, and at 6 months you can sit up.

1 YEAR

Every day, your brain cells make billions of new connections as your brain learns to control your body and understand the world. Your brain is growing faster than the rest of you, and your **head is huge** compared to your body. You start walking at 12–18 months, but at first your balance is poor and your large head makes you top-heavy and unstable.

18 MONTHS

You've practiced language almost since birth, **babbling** in the vowels and consonants you hear around you. By 18 months you can understand hundreds of words and probably say a handful. Your personality is beginning to show. Your parents will know whether you're shy or sociable, noisy or quiet, nervous or calm.

2 YEARS

Your brain is three-quarters adult size, and you are learning faster than at any time in your life. If you're an average 2-year-old, you can say about 300 words and speak in sentences, but you may be hard to understand. Your **sense of self** begins to develop: you can recognize yourself in a mirror or photograph, and you start to use the words "me" and "mine."

When did my *memory* begin?

When did I start telling *lies?*

How do I know what I'm *good* at?

How many *words* did I know at 3?

How did I *learn* to read?

3 YEARS

You're learning up to 10 new words a day and may already know 1,500 of the 40,000 or more you'll learn in your life. Your brain starts to lay down long-term **memories** that you can recall. Your sense of balance gets better, making you less clumsy. Over the next year or two you learn to run, hop, skip, catch balls, and tie shoelaces.

4 YEARS

Your **social skills** improve and you become aware of what other people are thinking. This makes you better at **lying** and deceiving people. Friendships become important, and you begin to see other children as individuals and play with them in a cooperative way. But you are very imaginative and can also play alone.

5 YEARS

Your brain is now almost adult-sized. You have probably started school, and begun to learn to read by understanding how letters work together to form words. You now have a store of long-term memories, including exciting times like vacations, Christmas, and your first day at school. But your memories go back only to age 3.

6–10 YEARS

During these years, you master tricky **physical skills** like cycling, swimming, skating, and ball handling. You also become skilled with your hands, making you better at writing, typing, and drawing. Your sense of identity grows. You start comparing yourself to others, and you become aware of what you're good at.

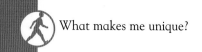

Why am I **clumsy**?

Why do my **moods** swing?

Why do I have such big **feet**?

Why am I changing **shape**?

11–12 YEARS

The years before the teens mark the beginning of **adolescence**—the period in which you change from child to adult. The point at which your sex organs start working is called **puberty**, and the age when this happens varies a great deal from person to person. Adolescence is a period of profound change—not just for your body but also for your brain.

GIRLS 13–17 YEARS

The female sex hormone **estrogen** is released by the ovaries. It causes a spurt of growth around age 11, and you may find yourself taller than boys of the same age for a couple of years. Once your periods start, you will grow no more than about 2.4 in (6 cm) taller. Puberty generally occurs at age 11 or 12, but it may be as early as age 8 or as late as 16. One of the main factors affecting the timing of puberty is your **weight**: girls start having periods when body weight reaches about 100 lb (45 kg).

- Your breasts start to develop.
- Your arms and legs get longer; your torso grows taller later.
- You start having periods.
- You grow pubic hair and, about two years after your periods start, hair grows under your arms.
- Your hips widen and continue to grow until your late teens.
- Your changing hormone levels are partly responsible for mood changes.
- You spend less time with family and more time with friends.
- You mix more with boys.
- You feel more **self-conscious**.

Am I a late developer?

Why am I so self-conscious?

Why do I have pimples?

Will I keep changing as I grow older?

BOYS 13–17 YEARS

18+ YEARS

The male sex hormone **testosterone** is released by the testes. It causes a spurt of growth around the age of 13, making you shoot up as much as 5 in (12 cm) in a single year. Growth happens from the **outside in**—first your hands and feet grow; then your arms and legs; then your torso. Bones grow faster than muscles, making you gangly, and your brain has to relearn how to balance your body, making you clumsy. Puberty is when you start making sperm, which happens on average when you are 13 or 14.

- You grow pubic hair.
- You start to produce sperm.
- Surges of testosterone can give you pimples (acne).
- Up to a third of boys develop slightly larger breasts in their early teens, before testosterone levels rise.
- Your voice deepens, often suddenly.
- About two years after pubic hair appears, hair grows on your face, legs, arms, and underarms.
- Your chest and shoulders broaden.
- Your face changes shape and your jaw becomes more square.
- Your body continues to fill out with muscle into your late teens.

By the time you reach your late teens, your brain and body stop changing so quickly, and you become more self-aware, independent, and socially confident. Your personality will continue to change throughout life as you develop a career, have relationships, and pursue your own interests.

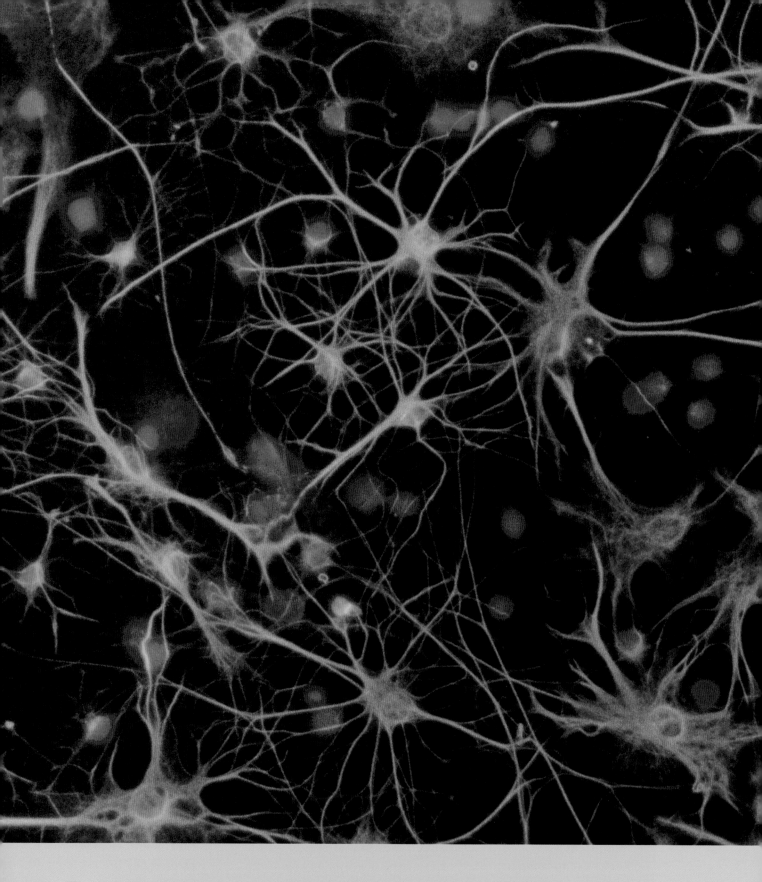

HOW DOES MY BRAIN WORK?

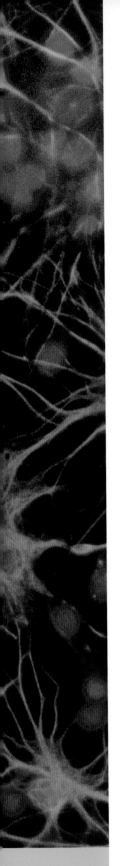

> ## The brain is the organ that creates the real you.

All your thoughts, emotions, and memories—as well as everything you see and feel—are conjured up inside this cabbage-sized lump of tissue.

Exactly how it works is a mystery, but its secret seems to lie in the way its 100 billion neurons connect together, forming a maze of electrical circuits more complicated than any computer. And unlike any computer, your brain is continually rewiring itself and changing as it learns.

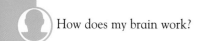

There are more possible circuits in

The **frontal lobe** is sometimes said to be the site of conscious thought, planning, and free will, but other parts of the brain also play a role in these functions.

FRONTAL

HOW DOES MY BRAIN WORK?

Your brain is pinkish-brown, about the size of two fists, and it has the consistency of gelatin. Its wrinkly surface is divided into **lobes**, which were once thought to specialize in different tasks, as organs do in the body. Although there's some truth in this, the brain is more complicated. It can spread tasks across lots of lobes and change the way it works if it's damaged.

One brain or two?

Each part of your brain is repeated on both sides, so you really have **two brains** in one. The two halves seem to have different characters and abilities, and they "talk" to each other. You need both halves to do many things. For instance, if you hear a joke, the left half understands the plot, but it's the right half that "gets" the joke.

your brain than atoms in the universe

The **parietal lobe** is important in movement, sensation, and orientation.

The **occipital lobe's** main job is to process information as it comes in from your eyes.

Cerebral cortex

The brain's wrinkly exterior is called the cerebral cortex. This is where **thinking** goes on, mainly at the front. Most of the rest of the cortex deals with information from your senses, especially vision and hearing. The cortex is split into left and right halves, each of which has four main lobes, as shown.

Cerebellum

The cerebellum helps to coordinate your body's **movement** and keep you balanced. But like most parts of the brain, it involves itself in lots of different tasks rather than specializing in one job. Recent discoveries show it plays a role in language, vision, reading, and planning.

Brain stem

At the very base of your brain is the brain stem, which is vital for basic life-support systems. It keeps your heart beating and your lungs breathing, and it helps control sleep and defecation. If your brain stem stops doing its job, you're said to be **brain-dead**.

LOBE

PARIETAL LOBE

TEMPORAL LOBE

OCCIPITAL LOBE

CEREBELLUM

BRAIN STEM

The **temporal lobe** deals with speech, language, and sound, among other tasks.

What's in the middle?

As a human, you have an amazingly big cerebral cortex, making your brain much smarter than that of any animal. Buried deep under the cortex, however, is what some people call your "animal brain"—the **limbic system**. This part of the brain generates basic emotions like fear and anger, and urges such as thirst and hunger.

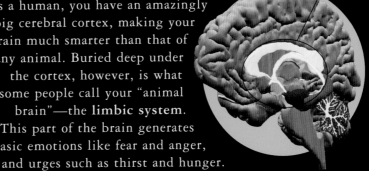

Limbic system

How much of what YOU think and do

What's the subconscious?

The psychoanalyst Sigmund Freud was wrong about a lot of things, but he did get one thing right: much of what we do is controlled by hidden forces in the brain, which he called **subconscious**. The subconscious mind works behind the scenes, and we aren't usually aware of it. When you ride a bike, for instance, your subconscious mind takes over the job of pedaling, steering, and so on, leaving your conscious mind free to think about other things.

Is my world the same as yours?

Your experience of the world is **completely private**. Nobody can ever experience your thoughts and sensations. Some philosophers think that each of us might actually see the world in very different ways. What you see as red, for example, might look blue to somebody else, though they would know it as red. But since we can never look into somebody else's thoughts, we'll never know if this is true.

Where do my THOUGHTS come from?

We all have a sense of **inner self** inside our brains. The inner self is the real "you"—it has your thoughts and feelings, it sees the world through your eyes, and it vanishes when you go to sleep. Your inner self seems to make all your decisions, but is it really **in control**?

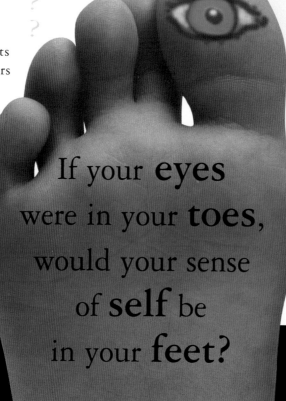

If your **eyes** were in your **toes**, would your sense of **self** be in your **feet**?

Where am I?

It feels like the inner self is just behind the eyes, but in fact there's no specific part of the brain that creates the feeling of a conscious self. Some experts say there may actually be two inner selves—a separate "you" in each half of your brain.

comes from hidden, subconscious forces?

Why do I daydream?

When you're bored or not concentrating, you'll quickly drift into an inner world and start to **daydream**.

Psychologists figure we spend up to 8 hours a day daydreaming

Like blinking, daydreaming happens all the time without our noticing it, and it probably has an important function. Most people have happy daydreams about things they want—like being rich and successful, **falling in love**, or becoming a hero. These positive daydreams can help focus your ambitions and motivate you. People often have **negative daydreams,** too, especially fantasies about taking revenge. These can be healthy because they help you let off steam.

What is consciousness?

The sensation of awareness that you feel while you're awake is called **consciousness**. Consciousness includes all the input from your senses, and it's dominated by vision—your top sense. It also includes the personal inner world that you can withdraw into and that nobody else can enter. Your thoughts, ideas, feelings, daydreams, and imagination are all part of consciousness.

FAQ

What's imagination?

Daydreams drift along without control, but you can also focus your thoughts and take control of the images in your mind. This happens when you use your imagination. For instance, try to remember how many rooms there are in your home. You can do this by imagining yourself walking through it.

What's my inner voice?

Thoughts sometimes take the form of an **inner voice** instead of images or feelings. When you're stuck on a difficult problem, you may even find yourself muttering as you speak your thoughts out loud. Talking to yourself like this doesn't mean you're crazy—it's just a good way of concentrating.

Everyone knows whether they're **right-handed** or **left-handed**, but do you know which is your dominant **foot**, your dominant **eye**, or your dominant **ear**? Because of the way your brain works, the two sides of your body are far from equal.

LEFT *or* RIGHT?

If you clasp your hands, cross your arms, or fold your legs, you'll probably always do it the same way, with either left or right on top. These asymmetries exist because your brain is split in two. The left half of your brain controls the right half of your body, and vice versa. For many tasks—whether physical or mental—one side of your brain is dominant.

IN MOST PEOPLE, THE LEFT BRAIN...

- is dominant for language, especially grammar, writing, and spelling
- is dominant for thinking logically
- is best at hearing the rhythm and pitch of music
- controls the right half of your body
- processes the right half of your vision

AND THE RIGHT BRAIN...

- is dominant at thinking spatially
- is best at appreciating music's melody
- is best at understanding jokes, sarcasm, and metaphors
- is best at recognizing objects
- controls the left half of your body
- processes the left half of your vision

◄ Which side of your BRAIN ► is the DOMINANT HALF?

Vision test

In many people, one half of the field of vision is dominant. Look directly at the nose in these two pictures. Does the girl look **happier** in one of them? Most people find the top face happier because the girl is smiling on the left, and the left half of the field of vision is usually dominant.

Which is your dominant foot?

Kick a soccer ball to see if you're right- or left-footed. About one in five people are left-footed. Many people are right-handed but left-footed.

Which is your dominant eye?

Hold up a finger and look past it to the distance. Close one eye at a time. The finger will jump with your weak eye and stay in place with your dominant eye.

WHICH HAND IS BEST?

What do **Bill Clinton**, **Paul McCartney**, and **Oprah Winfrey** have in common? Like 10 percent of the world's people, they are left-handed. Scientists have yet to figure out what causes people to become left- or right-handed. Identical twins are more likely to have the same preference, but the fact that they sometimes differ shows that genes aren't the only cause. Only babies can switch from one hand to the other, though by the age of two they develop a preference that sticks for life. Oddly, a lot of people aren't completely right-handed or left-handed. Some right-handers throw best with their left hand, for instance.

Most people are **right-mouthed**—they prefer to chew on the right side of the mouth

TEST YOUR HANDS

People who can use both hands are said to be **ambidextrous**. Take this test to see if you're ambidextrous. Hold a felt-tip pen

Left-hand start ↓

Right-hand start ↓

LOOK AT THESE FACES FOR 30 SECONDS, THEN TURN

MEMORY

FAQ

Where are memories stored?

There isn't one specific place in your brain where memories are stored. However, there is a part of the brain called the **hippocampus** (which is shaped like a seahorse) that plays a key role in memory, apparently turning short-term memories into long-term ones. If the hippocampus is damaged, people suffer from **amnesia**, which means they can't lay down new memories or recall the past.

Where were you when …

… the Army Public School in Peshawar, Pakistan, was attacked on December 16, 2014? Can you also remember who you were with and what you were doing when you heard the news? Our brains are especially good at remembering **shocking** events because the strong emotion makes the memory more vivid, more detailed, and easier to recall.

THE 4 TYPES OF MEMORY

SHORT-TERM

Shut your eyes and try to recite the last sentence you read. You're using your short-term memory. It last only **a few seconds** or minutes and then fades away, but it's vital for reading books and watching movies.

LONG-TERM

What did you get for your birthday? Now you're using long-term memory. Long-term memory can last for life. Strong **emotions**—such as joy or shock—can imprint permanent records in your long-term memory.

EPISODIC

Where did you go over summer vacation? Episodic memory is like a mental diary and has the **time and date** stamped on it. It includes whole experiences, including what you saw and how you felt.

FACTUAL

What's the world's tallest mountain? Now you're using your factual memory, which is a type of long-term memory. This is where you store what you learn in school. You need to keep **refreshing** your factual memories or they'll fade.

TO THE NEXT PAGE. CAN YOU SEE A NEW FACE?

Some memories fade with time, but others leave a permanent stamp on your brain. The first 3 years of your life are probably **blank**, but after that your memory began keeping careful records. Every experience you have leaves an impression somewhere in your brain, whether you can recall it or not.

HOW CAN I IMPROVE MY MEMORY?

There are lots of ways to improve your memory. One good way of memorizing schoolwork is to write notes as you read. This makes you concentrate on the most important facts, helping commit them to memory. Another effective technique is to reread your notes after a day, a week, and a month. Each time you refresh the memory, it becomes **easier to recall** and more permanent.

Memory tricks

Mnemonics are rhymes or phrases that help you commit facts to long-term memory. They work by linking boring information to something much more memorable. For instance, you can remember the order of the planets in the solar system with this mnemonic:

> ## " My very educated mother just served us noodles "

The first letter of each word stands for a planet, starting with the planet closest to the Sun: Mercury, Venus, Earth, Mars, Jupiter, Saturn, Uranus, Neptune.

To remember a list of numbers, convert each number into a mental image of a rhyming object, such as these:

1 bun
2 shoe
3 tree
4 door
5 hive
6 sticks
7 heaven
8 gate
9 wine
10 hen

Then combine the objects in an **imaginary scene**. For instance, to remember the year 1066, think of a hen with a pair of sticks poking out of its ears!

FAQ

I'm sorry—I forgot!

Forgetting is just as important as remembering. If your brain didn't forget, your memory would become clogged with irrelevant details and you wouldn't be able to think straight. So your brain usually filters out only **interesting** or **unusual** information and discards everything else.

Do some people have photographic memory?

Some people perform amazing feats of memory, such as recalling the sequence of all the cards in a deck after only one glance. But they don't have photographic memory—they've just trained themselves to use lots of clever memory tricks. Photographic memory probably doesn't exist.

CAN YOU SPOT THE NEW FACE? Your brain has a built-in

Test your MEMORY

TRY THESE TESTS TO SEE HOW GOOD YOUR MEMORY IS

1 **How's your memory for words?**
- Study the 12 words below for 30 seconds exactly.
- Close the book, wait a minute, and try to write them all down.
- Check how well you did and go to page 96 to see what your results mean.

Tip: visualizing the words and combining the images may help.

paper   salad   cup
          carrot   vinegar
chair   vomit
          carpet   dust
pebble   jam   camel

7 2 8 3 4 5

Numbers can be harder to remember than

ability to recognize faces, so you should find this test fairly easy.

2 How's your visual memory?

- Study the objects on the tray for 30 seconds exactly.
- Close the book, wait a minute, and try to write down all the objects you saw.
- Check how well you did and go to page 96 to see what your results mean.

Tip: sketching the tray from memory may help.

736
words or images

3 Number cruncher

- Give yourself 15 seconds to memorize the number on the left.
- Close the book, wait a minute, then write it down.
- Check your result and see page 96.

Tip: keep saying the number to yourself.

FAQ

When do I learn the most?

You learn some things best at certain ages—during **critical periods**. The critical period for **learning to see** is the first year of life. If a baby's eyes don't work properly during its first year, it may end up permanently blind, even if the eyes get better. The critical period for **learning to speak** is the first 11 years of life. You can learn to speak any language fluently during this period.

Why does practice make perfect?

Physical skills like ice-skating or driving a car involve a special type of learning that uses a part of the brain called the cerebellum. When you start learning a tricky physical skill, you have to think hard about how to move each muscle. You use your cerebral cortex to consciously move your body, which takes concentration. After **practice**, however, the movements become second nature. Your cerebellum learns to take over, controlling your body like an autopilot.

Can I change my BRAIN?

Your brain is **plastic**—it learns and adapts not by changing its software, as a computer does, but by physically changing its hardware. You were born with nearly all your 100 billion brain cells in place, but the **connections** between those cells can alter throughout life. Your brain learns by changing the connections and rewiring itself, creating endless new circuits.

The people you meet, the places you visit, the things you see, the skills you learn, even the dreams you have—all these things can change the **physical structure** of your brain. Your experience in life leaves its mark in the tangled web of connections inside your brain.

Since nobody has exactly the same life as you, nobody has a brain quite like yours

Your brain grows stronger

Whenever you learn a new skill or commit something to memory, you force your brain to rewire itself. And each time you practice the skill or refresh your memory, you make the new circuits **slightly stronger**, like wearing a path through a field.

When does my brain change most?

Your brain changes throughout life, but there are some periods when the rate of change is especially fast. In the first 2 or 3 years of life, a baby's brain cells grow connections at an amazing rate. But from the age of 3 onward, the brain starts pruning back, getting rid of connections it doesn't need and **killing brains cells** that don't get used. Another spurt of growth in connections happens at age 11–12, just before puberty. During adolescence, the new connections are pruned back once again.

Can I exercise my brain?

In some ways, your brain is like a **muscle**. If you exercise certain parts a lot, they grow stronger. Scientists have found that in violinists, a larger-than-usual area of brain is devoted to control of the left hand, which has the fiddly job of pressing the violin's strings while the right arm swings the bow. Likewise, in blind people who read Braille, an unusually large area of the brain is allocated to touch.

FAQ

Does sleep help me learn?

If you're trying to crack a tricky level in a computer game or master a difficult piano piece, you might find it easier to sleep on it and come back in the morning. Neuroscientists think there's a link between sleep and learning, especially for physical skills that require practice. There's also evidence that sleep can help you solve mental challenges, such as mathematical puzzles.

Stay focused

Learning is all about **attention**. Your brain takes in information only when it is interested and paying attention. If you get tired or bored and start to drift away, you stop learning.

Can the brain repair itself?

People who suffer brain damage after a stroke or injury often make what seems to be a **miraculous recovery**. A stroke can leave you paralyzed and unable to speak, yet several months later you can be walking and talking again. This happens because the brain is plastic. If the speech center in the left side of the brain is damaged, for instance, the right side of the brain can learn to do the same job.

FAQ

What's IQ?

The IQ (intelligence quotient) test is the most famous way of measuring intelligence. It tests your spatial, verbal, and numerical skills and gives an overall score. The IQ test was originally devised to spot children who are struggling in school. It can give a good indication of how well you might do at school, but it doesn't necessarily show how successful you will be in life.

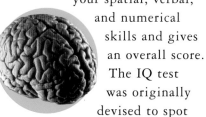

Is IQ genetic?

Studies of identical twins suggest that, among children brought up in stable, wealthy homes, most of the variation in IQ is related to **genes**. However, among children who grow up in underprivileged homes, most of the variation in IQ is caused by the **environment**. Though the results look contradictory, they show that genes and environment **both** have an influence on your IQ.

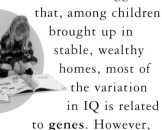

Am I a GENIUS?

WHAT ARE YOU BEST AT?

Intelligence can mean lots of different things, such as how good you are at math or how well you express yourself with words. The tests on the next few pages will give you an idea of what you might be best at.

SPATIAL intelligence

Thinking spatially means being able to see shapes in your **mind's eye** and turn them around. This type of intelligence is very useful in understanding machines and reading maps. On average, boys score higher than girls at spatial thinking.

VERBAL intelligence

This is a measure of your reading and writing skills. People with high verbal intelligence can read quickly and **take in information** easily. They can also express themselves well in writing. On average, girls score higher at this test than boys.

It takes 10,000 HOURS of

Is a smart person merely someone who knows lots of **facts**, or is intelligence about solving **logic puzzles** or being **imaginative**? And is it something you're born with or something you develop through practice?

NUMERICAL intelligence

High numerical intelligence is a sign of a logical, analytical mind. If you find math easy, you probably have high numerical intelligence. Some people score highly at this despite a low score for verbal intelligence.

LATERAL intelligence

Thinking laterally means using your **imagination** to solve a puzzle that may not have a logical answer. Lateral-thinking puzzles can be very difficult. If you're good at them, you probably have a very **creative** mind.

EMOTIONAL intelligence

If you're good at understanding how other people feel and think, you may have a high emotional IQ. People with high emotional IQ often become very successful in life, even if they score low on other types of intelligence tests.

FAQ

Can I change my IQ?

Your IQ isn't set in stone. If you study hard in school, your IQ will **go up**. The average IQ of whole nations has gone up over the last century, probably because of improvements in education. In Japan, average IQ has gone up about 12 points in the last 50 years. The change shows yet again that the environment can have a big impact on IQ.

What makes a genius?

A genius is someone who becomes exceptionally talented in a subject. **Albert Einstein** was perhaps the greatest scientific genius of all time. When he died, experts cut open his brain to see what was special about it, but it looked like any other brain. Even stranger, Einstein did badly at school and hated his teacher. His secret was probably his obsessive interest in science. **Obsession** is one thing that all geniuses have in common, and it often starts in childhood.

practice to become an *expert*

SPATIAL *intelligence* test

Try out this test, allowing yourself 20 minutes to complete it. Go to page 96 to check your answers.

1 If you want to cut a pizza into 8 equal portions, how many cuts do you need to make across it?
a) 8
b) 2
c) 16
d) 6
e) 4

2 How many edges does a cube have?
a) 8
b) 12
c) 16
d) 6
e) 4

3 Which shape matches the gray shape?

 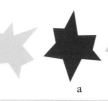 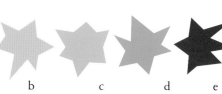

a b c d e

4 Which circle is the odd one out?

 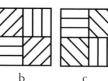

a b c d e

5 Which square is the odd one out?

a b c d e

VERBAL *intelligence* test

Try out this test, allowing yourself 20 minutes to complete it. Go to page 96 to check your answers.

1 India is to Asia as Italy is to
a) America
b) Africa
c) Europe
d) pizza
e) Jupiter

2 Ice is to water as solid is to
a) gas
b) ice
c) metal
d) liquid
e) vapor

3 Foot is to distance as pound is to
a) weight
b) gram
c) pound
d) ton
e) foot

4 Gigantic is to miniature as joyful is to
a) happy
b) ecstatic
c) bored
d) miserable
e) flea

5 Banana is to apple as cabbage is to

6 Which word is the odd one out?

7 Which word is the odd one out?

8 Which word is the odd one out?

6 Which of the objects on the bottom line comes next in the sequence?

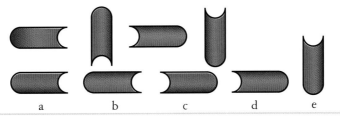

a   b   c   d   e

7 Which blue key fits the red shape?

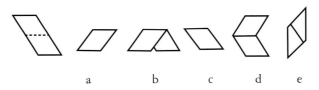

a   b

c   d   e

8 Which shape completes the sequence?

is to   as   is to...

a   b   c   d   e

9 What shape is formed by folding the paper along the dotted line?

a   b   c   d   e

10 Which work of art contains the pattern below?

a

b

c

d

e

9 Which word is the odd one out?

a) agree
b) dispute
c) contradict
d) argue
e) disagree

10 Which word is the odd one out?

a) horse
b) cow
c) kangaroo
d) donkey
e) goat

11 Which word has a meaning similar to "construct"?

a) destroy
b) tower
c) brick
d) build
e) bridge

12 Which word has a meaning similar to "diverse"?

a) similar
b) spider
c) varied
d) calamity
e) abacus

13 Which word has a meaning similar to "essential"?

a) extra
b) harmonica
c) oil
d) surplus
e) vital

14 Which word has a meaning similar to "rotate"?

a) spin
b) encircle
c) invert
d) flip
e) collapse

15 If some gleebs are squmps, and some squmps are noomies, then some gleebs are definitely noomies. This statement is
a) true
b) false
c) sometimes true
d) sometimes false
e) none of the above

16 A cynic is someone who knows the price of everything and the _____ of nothing.

a) size
b) value
c) meaning
d) circumference
e) opposite

NUMERICAL *intelligence* test

NUMERICAL *intelligence* test

Try this test to see if you're good at numerical thinking. Allow yourself 30 minutes, then go to page 96 to check your answers. Be careful not to rush—it's harder than the other tests, and there are a few trick questions!

1 A farmer builds a 10-yard (or 10-meter) fence by stringing wire between wooden posts placed 2 yards (or meters) apart. How many posts does he need?
a) 10
b) 2
c) 4
d) 5
e) 6

2 The sum of all numbers from 1 to 7 is
a) 8
b) 15
c) 22
d) 25
e) 28

3 The day after tomorrow is two days before Tuesday. What day is it today?
a) Friday
b) Saturday
c) Sunday
d) Monday
e) Tuesday

4 What number comes next in the following sequence?

1, 2, 3, 5, 8, 13...
a) 15
b) 17
c) 19
d) 21
e) 23

5 If two cooks can peel two potatoes in one minute, how many cooks will it take to peel 20 potatoes in 10 minutes?
a) 1
b) 2
c) 3
d) 4
e) 5

6 1985516 is to sheep as 2315126 is to
a) wolf
b) horse
c) antelope
d) goat
e) cattle

LATERAL *intelligence*

LATERAL *thinking* test

You need to use your imagination to do this test. The questions are hard, so ask someone to help you if you're stuck. Don't be surprised if you get most of them wrong! Answers on page 96.

1 I live alone in a small house with no doors or windows, and when I leave I must break through the walls. What am I?

2 It's spring. You see a carrot and two pieces of coal together in somebody's front yard. How did they get there?

3 A man is lying dead in a field next to a backpack. How did he get there?

4 Two babies are born at the same time on the same day in the same month in the same year at the same hospital to the same biological mother. Why are they not twins?

7 Brian and Kevin collected 30 snails in a garden. Brian found five times more snails than Kevin. How many snails did Kevin find?

a) 6
b) 8
c) 3
d) none
e) 5

8 You're running in a race and you pass the person in second place. What place are you in now?

a) last
b) 4th
c) 3rd
d) 2nd
e) 1st

9 Jessica is taller than Nicole, and Maria is shorter than Jessica. Which of the following statements is correct?

a) Maria is taller than Nicole
b) Maria is shorter than Nicole
c) Maria is as tall as Nicole
d) It's impossible to tell
e) Maria is Nicole's sister

10 A group of ducks are walking in a line. There are two ducks in front of a duck, two ducks behind a duck, and a duck in the middle. How many ducks are there?

a) 1
b) 5
c) 3
d) 7
e) 2

11 What number is one-half of one-fourth of one-tenth of 800?

a) 2
b) 5
c) 8
d) 10
e) 40

12 The train trip from Centerville to Fairview is 300 miles. A fast train leaves Fairview at the same time as a slow train leaves Centerville. If the fast train goes at twice the speed of the slow train, how many miles will the slow train have traveled when they pass?

a) 100 miles
b) 150 miles
c) 200 miles
d) 133 miles
e) 266 miles

13 David is 4 years old and his sister Sarah is three times older. When David is 12 years old, how old will Sarah be?

a) 16
b) 20
c) 24
d) 28
e) 36

14 What number comes next in the following sequence?

144, 121, 100, 81, 64...

a) 55
b) 49
c) 36
d) 16
e) 9

15 A car travels 23 miles in 30 minutes. How fast it is traveling?

a) 23 mph
b) 30 mph
c) 46 mph
d) 52 mph
e) 60 mph

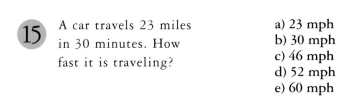

5 Why is it better for utility covers to be round instead of square?
Clue: think about turning them.

6 A man went to a party and drank some of the punch. He then left early. Everyone else at the party who drank the punch subsequently died of poisoning. Why did the man not die?
Clue: there was poison in the punch.

7 What's more powerful than God; the rich need it, the poor have it, and if you eat it you'll die?
Clue: the answer is a word.

8 Three switches in the basement are wired to three lights in a room upstairs. How can you determine which switch turns on which light with just one trip from the basement to the room?
Clue: there are light bulbs in the lights.

9 A man lives on the tenth floor of a building. Every day he takes the elevator to the ground floor to go to work. When he returns, he takes the elevator to the seventh floor and walks the rest of the way. If it's raining, he takes the elevator all the way up. Why?
Clue: he owns an umbrella.

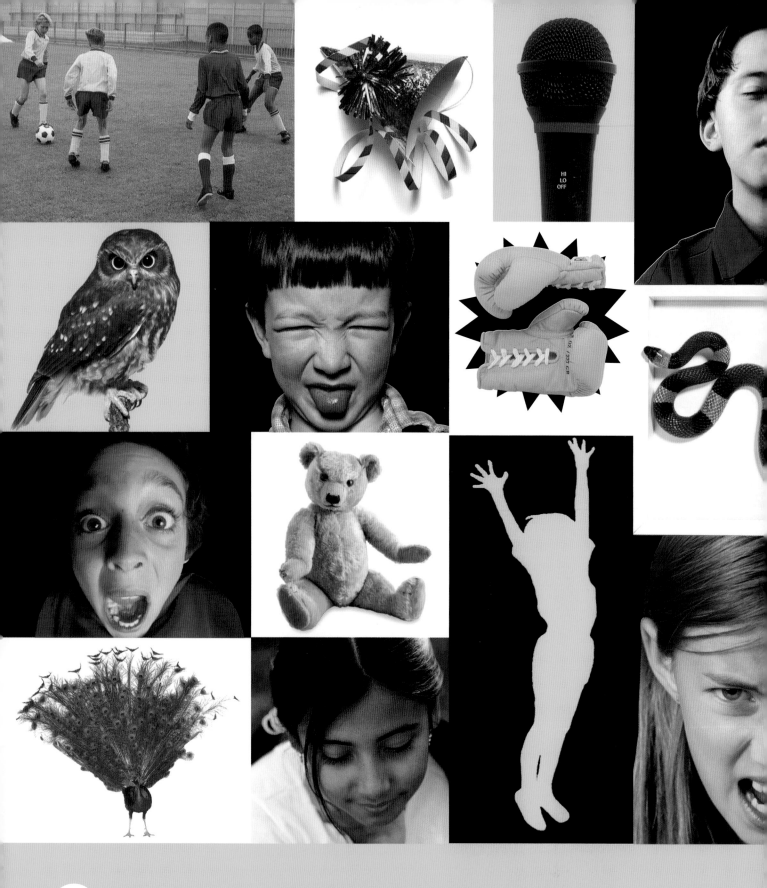

WHAT KIND OF PERSON AM I?

THE BIG FIVE

One of the most common tests psychologists use to study personality is the **Big Five** test, which breaks down personality into the five dimensions below. These dimensions are independent, which means that your score in one dimension has no bearing on the others.

You might be very extroverted, for instance, but quite disagreeable

To do the Big Five test properly, you need to work through questionnaires designed by psychologists. The test on the previous page can only give you a hint at your true scores, so don't worry if the results seem disappointing.

Is personality in the genes?

Studies of identical twins suggest that genes do have a big influence on everyone's personality. In one major study, genes accounted for about **40 percent** of the variation in people's Big Five scores, and the environment accounted for about **35 percent** of the variation. (The remaining 25 percent was due to sampling error.)

personality traits

AGREEABLENESS

Agreeableness is a measure of how easy you are to get along with. If you scored highly, people probably find you cooperative and **good-natured**. If you got a low score, you might be too outspoken or argumentative sometimes. People tend to become more agreeable as they get older.

OPENNESS

If you're very open, you like **new experiences** and change. You make decisions on the spur of the moment rather than following plans, and you tend to dip into things rather than immersing yourself in one hobby. People who score low on openness prefer familiar surroundings and routines, and they may become highly absorbed in one hobby.

FAQ

Can I change?

If you think you have a bad personality, don't panic. Personality changes during life, even in adulthood. In your 20s and 30s, your agreeableness and conscientiousness will probably go up. In women, neuroticism and extroversion go down with age. In men they stay the same, though they start off lower.

What job will suit me?

Different careers suit different personalities. If you're very shy, you may be happier in a career that's task-oriented rather than people-oriented. Understanding your personality can help you identify your **strengths** and work out which career might suit you best. But remember that people change; many people overcome shyness as they grow older, for instance.

Does birth order matter?

Some people say your position in a family has a strong influence on personality. The **oldest child**, for instance, often seems to be the most sensible, while younger children are more likely to be risk-takers. Careful study, however, suggests that these effects apply only **within the family**. When you're away from home and with friends, the way you behave has nothing to do with your family's birth order.

69

FAQ

Why am I shy?

Introverts can feel awkward or nervous in social situations, and this can make them avoid other people. There's nothing wrong with feeling shy—it's an important defensive **instinct**. Everybody feels shy from time to time, though most people become good at hiding it and acting confident as they get older. People also become less shy and more socially skilled as they grow out of their teens and start feeling less self-conscious.

Are you an ambivert?

Most people aren't complete extroverts or introverts. They're **ambiverts**, which means they're somewhere in the middle. An ambivert might be shy with strangers but very confident and outgoing with friends and family.

How many friends should you have?

Many people worry about how **popular** they are, especially during their teens. Extroverts always seem to be surrounded by a crowd of friends, while introverts might spend their time with just one best friend. There's no right answer to how many friends you should have—all that matters is that you enjoy spending time together.

One way of thinking about your personality is to decide whether you're an **extrovert** *or* an **introvert**. Do you devote your attention to the outer world of people and activities or

Introvert

OR

IF YOU'RE AN INTROVERT, YOU ARE...

- Quiet and reserved
- Serious and cautious
- Sensitive and reflective
- Happy on your own

Introverts tend to **think things through** before talking and acting, and are good at listening to others. They are shy and quiet, which sometimes makes them seem **aloof** or unfriendly. Introverts do well in jobs that involve working independently, thinking carefully, and analyzing information.

the inner world of ideas and experiences? Do you crave **excitement** and company, or do you prefer spending time on your own, away from the crowd?

EXTROVERT

IF YOU'RE AN EXTROVERT, YOU ARE...

- Outgoing and communicative
- Adventurous and risk-taking
- Confident and assertive
- Easily bored

Extroverts are energized by others. They are confident and **make friends easily**, and they can be great fun. Sometimes, however, extroverts can come across as shallow or loud. Extroverts do well in active jobs that involve meeting lots of people, and they can make **great leaders**.

FAQ

Are you a party animal?

Extroverts love going to **parties** and socializing with lots of new people. The "life and soul of a party" is much more likely to be an extrovert than an introvert. Extroverts are confident talkers and quickly get to know people, which can make them popular. But, like introverts, they probably have only a few friends who are really close.

Are you a thrill-seeker?

Some psychologists think extroverts have a gene that makes them **less sensitive** to stimulation than introverts. According to this theory, introverts are so easily stimulated that they can find social situations stressful, so they shy away from people. Extroverts, in contrast, seek out stimulation to avoid getting bored. So extroverts are more likely to be thrill-seekers who take part in dangerous sports, like skydiving or bungee jumping.

TAKE THE LEMON JUICE TEST

To see if you're more introverted than a friend, drop some **lemon juice** on both your tongues and then collect your **saliva** in glasses. Introverts tend to make more saliva than extroverts because they are more sensitive to stimulation.

FAQ

Do male and female brains look different?

Men have slightly bigger brains than women, even allowing for their larger bodies, but the average IQ of men and women is the same. In women, the connection between the two halves of the brain is a little thicker. Some people say this means women are better at using both sides of the brain together.

What's testosterone?

The male sex hormone testosterone, which triggers puberty in boys, has a big impact on behavior and personality. When animals are given extra testosterone, they become more **aggressive** and **competitive**. Testosterone has the same effect in humans, making boys generally more aggressive and competitive.

Take the finger test

Testosterone is present in the body throughout life, in girls as well as boys. It even affects the way an unborn baby develops. If you had a high level of fetal testosterone, your **ring finger** may be longer than your index finger, and you're more likely to have a **male brain**.

index finger   ring finger

What SEX is

IF YOU HAVE A FEMALE BRAIN, YOU'RE GOOD AT:

- skills that use the **left side** of your brain, such as language, reading, and writing
- understanding people's feelings
- telling when someone is lying
- reading body language
- noticing the bigger picture

You might be a girl who's good at male skills like fixing computers, or you might be a boy with good social skills

Psychologists think male and female brains have different skills. The differences are not huge or absolute—they are based on **averages**. On average, female brains are better at **empathizing** skills, such as understanding people's feelings. On average, male brains are better at **systemizing** skills, such as understanding how machines work. And these differences seem to be present from birth—they don't occur just because boys and girls are brought up differently.

If you have a BALANCED BRAIN you are

my BRAIN?

IF YOU HAVE A MALE BRAIN, YOU'RE BETTER AT:

- skills that use the **right side** of the brain, such as thinking about shapes or understanding maps and diagrams
- understanding technical matters
- memorizing lists of facts
- noticing small details

Generalizations can be misleading because very very few people are perfectly average

Gender is a bit like a **spectrum**, with the typical male brain at one end and the typical female brain at the other. Where you fall on the spectrum depends on your own skills and abilities. Most people are somewhere in the middle, where male and female skills **overlap**. As a result, you might have a mix of typically male and typically female skills. You might have great social skills, for instance, but also be good at fixing computers. Then again, you might be hopeless at both.

FAQ

Am I a people person?
If you're good at understanding people and putting them at ease, you're a people person. This is a typically female skill. Some scientists think evolution has given women better social skills (on average) because they tend to spend more time than men caring for children and families.

The extreme male brain
Some people seem to have an exaggerated type of male brain, with very poor social skills but sometimes enhanced systemizing skills. Such people are said to be **autistic**. Autistic children have difficulties relating to other people, and they sometimes develop obsessive interests in unusual subjects, such as memorizing car license plates or copying pictures perfectly.

AZN 885

The bike test
To find out how male someone's brain is, ask them to **draw a bike** from memory in only 30 seconds. Men tend to draw accurate bikes, like the blue one. Women are more likely to draw bikes that couldn't possibly work, like the pink one, but might include a rider.

equally good at **MALE** and **FEMALE** skills

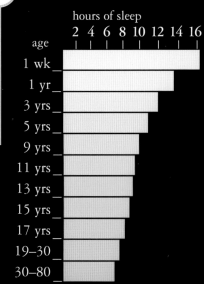

hours of sleep

age	2 4 6 8 10 12 14 16
1 wk	
1 yr	
3 yrs	
5 yrs	
9 yrs	
11 yrs	
13 yrs	
15 yrs	
17 yrs	
19–30	
30–80	

How much is enough?

As the chart above shows, you need less sleep as you get older. Teenagers need about **two hours more** than adults and suffer much more from the effects of sleep deprivation. So don't be surprised if you find it hard to get out of bed in the morning!

What's the point of sleep?

IF YOU'RE AN OWL, YOU...

- Sleep through your alarm clock
- Stay awake well past midnight
- Enjoy sleeping in

Are *you* an OWL

If you find it hard to get out of bed in the morning, it doesn't necessarily mean you're lazy—it could be down to your genes. Your genes have a big influence on how much

IF YOU'RE A LARK, YOU...

- Jump out of bed early in the morning
- Don't like staying up late
- Fall asleep easily

OR a LARK?

The length of the clock varies from person to person and depends partly on your **genes**. On average, it's 24 hours 18 minutes (maybe that's why most people always want more sleep in the mornings). If your clock is short, you're a **lark**—someone who's full of energy early in the day. If your clock is long, you're an **owl**—and you probably like staying up late.

Can I reset my clock?

When you fly across the world, your body clock goes haywire, giving you **jet lag**. The clock no longer matches the true time, so you have to reset it. Bright light can help. When light enters your eyes, it triggers a signal that tells your brain it's daytime. Likewise, darkness tells your brain that it's night—and time to release the hormones that help you sleep.

Am I sleep-deprived?

It should take 10–15 minutes to fall asleep. It if takes less, you're **sleep-deprived**, which means you aren't getting enough sleep. Sleep deprivation makes you miserable and **bad-tempered**, slows your learning, and can even cause hallucinations. If you're sleep-deprived at school, you might nod off in class. Sleep-deprived drivers can fall asleep at the wheel and crash.

TAKE THE TEST

1 When your alarm clock wakes you up, do you:

a. Get out of bed right away?

b. Switch it off and get up slowly?

c. Put the alarm clock on snooze?

d. Switch it off and go back to sleep?

2 What time do you go to bed on Friday evenings?

a. 8:00–9:00 pm

b. 9:00–10:00 pm

c. 10:00–11:00 pm

d. after 11:00 pm

3 What time do you get up on Saturday mornings?

a. before 9:00 am

b. 9:00–10:00 am

c. 10:00–11:00 am

d. after 11:00 am

4 How hungry are you when you eat breakfast?

a. Very hungry

b. Only slightly hungry

c. Not really hungry but you make an effort to eat

d. Disgusted by the thought of food

5 At what time of day do you feel most energetic?

a. Mornings

b. Afternoons

c. Evenings

d. Late at night

6 How quickly do you usually fall asleep?

a. In 10 minutes

b. 10–20 minutes

c. 20–30 minutes

d. More than 30 minutes

See page 96 to get your results.

FAQ

What are nightmares?

The part of your brain that creates **emotions** is very active in dreams. If it creates a feeling of fear, the dream becomes a **nightmare**, and the rest of your brain makes up a story to go with it.

You might think you're falling from a height or trying to escape and hide from something scary, for instance. Nightmares are natural and everyone has them, but they get less common as you get older.

Why don't I know I'm dreaming?

One of the odd things about dreams is that when you're in one, you can't tell it's a dream—even though the strangest things keep happening. This is because you have no sense of **self-awareness** in dreams. Your brain's frontal lobes, which create your sense of self, are mostly shut down.

Do animals dream?

Many animals experience REM sleep, so perhaps they dream as well. Oddly, the amount of time they spend in REM sleep depends on how immature they are at birth. The **platypus**, which is tiny and helpless at birth, appears to dream for **8 hours** a day. Dolphins and dream, and birds seem to dream in song—their brain waves in sleep are the same as when they sing.

Why do I DREAM?

Dreams can be **terrifying**, bizarre, and fantastic, but what in the world are they for? Despite decades of research, dreams remain one of the brain's biggest mysteries.

When do I dream?

When you sleep, your brain goes through cycles of activity, alternating between **deep** and **shallow** sleep every 90 minutes. Most of your dreams happen in the shallow part of the cycle, when you're nearly awake. During these shallow periods, your **eyes dart around** under your eyelids as though you're watching something. This is called REM (rapid eye movement) sleep. If you wake someone in REM sleep, there's an 80 percent chance that they'll remember being in a dream.

REM sleep ●
Light sleep ●
Deep sleep ●

AWAKE · ASLEEP

hours 1 2 3 4 5 6 7 8

How much do I dream?

Most people don't realize how much they dream. There are two good reasons for this. First, unless you wake in a dream, you won't remember anything about it. And second, **dreams distort time**. If someone splashes your face to wake you, you might wake up thinking you've been dreaming of rain for hours. Sleep scientists think we dream about five times a night and spend 1–2 **hours** in dreams. Most dreams happen in REM sleep, but some people think we can dream in deeper sleep as well.

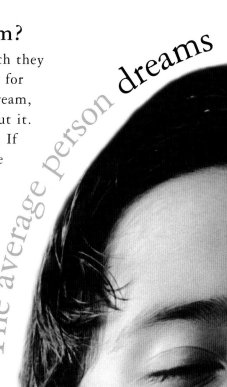

The average person dreams

You'll spend around five years of your life in dreams

Do dreams have a purpose?

There are lots of theories about why we dream, but the truth is that nobody really knows. Some experts think dreams help lay down **memories**, but there are people who never dream and have perfectly good memories. Other experts say dreams help sort out the experiences of the day, but unborn babies spend nearly half their time in REM sleep, and they have no experiences to sort out. And if dreams are simply for sorting information, why are they so **strange**?

What do my dreams mean?

The psychoanalyst **Sigmund Freud** thought dreams were a window into our hidden, **unconscious** desires, and he spent years talking to patients about their dreams and thinking up complicated meanings for them. Most people now think Freud read too much into dreams. The strange events in a dream might just be **meaningless** stories that your brain invents out of memories because it's active but starved of input from the senses.

Can I move during a dream?

When you dream, your body is literally **paralyzed**. This is a safety feature to stop you from acting out your dreams. Your brain keeps sending messages to your muscles to try to move them, but your **spinal cord** blocks the messages. Messages do still get through to your eyes, lungs, and heart, though, and that's why your eyes dart around and your heart rate and breathing become irregular. Sometimes people partially wake from dreams while still paralyzed and find themselves pinned to the bed, unable to move and **utterly terrified**.

about 1,825 times a year

FAQ

What's the lurch?

Have you ever dreamed that you're falling, only to wake with a lurch just before you hit the ground? This happens most often when you're right on the verge of falling asleep, and it's called a **hypnagogic startle**. It's caused by your brain suddenly waking again.

Why do people sleepwalk?

Some people get out of bed and walk around when they are fast asleep—they are **sleepwalking**. Sleepwalkers are not acting out their dreams. In fact, they are not dreaming at all. Sleepwalking usually happens as a cycle of very deep sleep comes to an end. Many people move around in bed or mumble at this point, but sleepwalkers get up and walk around. Sleep scientists call it a **partial awakening** because the brain is half awake and half asleep.

Keep a dream diary

Dreams are hard to remember, but if you write them down as soon as you wake up, your notes will help you recall them later. Try to answer these questions by writing down your dreams:

- Do you dream in color?
- Can you hear in dreams?
- Can you control dreams?
- Can you fly in dreams?
- What emotions do you feel?
- Can you sense time?

Can you control your EMOTIONS?

FEAR

Fear makes the eyebrows shoot up and pulls up the eyelids, exposing the whites of the eyes above the iris. At the same time, the lower eyelids rise. The mouth opens with a gasp and the lips pull back tensely. Blood drains from the skin, making it turn pale.

ANGER

Muscles pull the eyebrows down and inward, causing vertical wrinkles to appear between them. The eyes narrow and take on a **glaring** expression that doesn't waver. The mouth may close tightly or open and snarl with rage, exposing the teeth. Blood rushes to the face, making it red.

JOY

A true smile affects the whole face, raising the cheeks and making crow's feet appear beside the eyes and bags appear under them. The mouth opens and the top lip pulls back, exposing the upper teeth. Smiling also sends **feedback signals** to the brain, intensifying the feeling of joy.

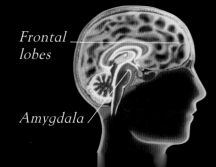

Frontal lobes

Amygdala

Temper, temper!

Strong emotions are triggered by a part of the brain called the **amygdala**, in the limbic system. More advanced parts of the brain called the **frontal lobes** act as policemen, enabling us to hide emotions and resist the urge to act on them. The frontal lobes take a long time to develop and don't reach maturity until we are in our twenties. As a result, children and teenagers are prone to **tantrums** and flashes of temper. Their amygdalas generate strong feelings, but their frontal lobes are not sufficiently mature to control them.

The way we show **emotions** in our faces is the same **all over the world**—a smile means the same thing in the Sahara Desert or the Amazon jungle. Psychologists think there are 6 primary emotions, each with a characteristic facial expression. These facial expressions are **programmed** into our brains by our genes.

Like primary colors, emotions mix together.

SURPRISE SADNESS DISGUST

Surprise can look similar to fear, but there are subtle differences. The eyebrows not only shoot up but become strongly arched. The jaw drops open, making the mouth look slack, and the eyes widen, exposing their whites. Surprise is difficult to hide, but fear can be masked.

In a sad face, the ends of the mouth droop and the inner ends of the eyebrows rise, creating a triangular shape above the nose, often with wrinkles higher up. The eyes may water or redden in preparation for tears, but often a sad person will turn away or cover their face to hide this telltale sign.

When a person feels intensely disgusted, strong wrinkles spread across the bridge of the nose and forehead. The eyes narrow, eyebrows come down, and cheeks rise. The sight of intense disgust in someone's face can also trigger a **feeling** of disgust in anyone watching.

Keep a feelings diary

Your emotions may not always be accurate: you may be highly strung and overreact sometimes. Try this exercise to find out how reliable your emotions are.

- Next time you have a strong feeling about something, try to work out exactly what the feeling is and what caused it. Write your conclusions in a "feelings diary." Keep doing this every time you feel strongly.
- After a few days, look back at what you've written. Were your feelings justified? Write down any comments in your diary.
- After two or three weeks, review your diary. Were your feelings accurate or were you overreacting? Were some feelings

What makes you AFRAID?

Powerful emotions like fear, anger, surprise, and disgust are basic **instincts** that protect you from danger and help you survive. They don't just affect your state of mind—they prime your whole body for action by triggering a state known as **arousal**. This happens so amazingly quickly that your body is on red alert before you even have time to think about what's happening.

SEE

REACT

FEEL

THINK

HOW DOES **FEAR** AFFECT THE BODY?

Your digestive system is put on hold and blood rushes away from it to supply your muscles, giving you butterflies in the stomach. Adrenaline also stimulates your bowels. In wild animals, this reflex causes weight loss to help the animal flee.

Your eyes widen and appear to flash.

Blood rushes to your muscles.

Your breathing rate suddenly rises, making you gasp for air.

Your heart speeds up with a jolt, making your chest pound. The faster heart rate helps deliver extra oxygen to your muscles.

THE FIRST SECOND

Fear is the most powerful emotion of all. Lightning reactions are vital, so the fear pathway takes a **shortcut** through your brain, bypassing consciousness. This is what happens in the first split second, as you freeze in terror:

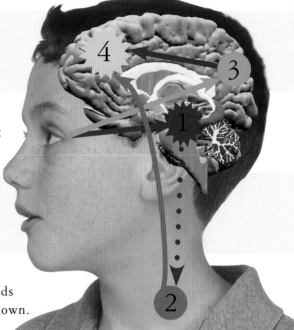

1 A signal passes from your eyes or ears to your **limbic system**, which makes a very quick analysis and sends a danger signal to your body.

2 Your body is put on red alert by the nervous system and the hormone **adrenaline**. The body sends feedback signals to your **frontal lobes**, making you feel fear.

3 A slower signal from your eyes or ears goes to your **sensory cortex**, which works out what you've really seen and sends a message to your frontal lobes.

4 The frontal lobes use **thought** and **memory** to decide whether the threat is truly dangerous. If it isn't, it sends signals to the limbic system to make your body calm down.

Fear has a profound and instant effect on your whole body. It increases your level of arousal by stimulating your **sympathetic nervous system**. This gets your heart, lungs, and muscles ready for action. The hormone **adrenaline** has the same effect, but it lingers in your blood, making you feel shaken after the moment of danger passes.

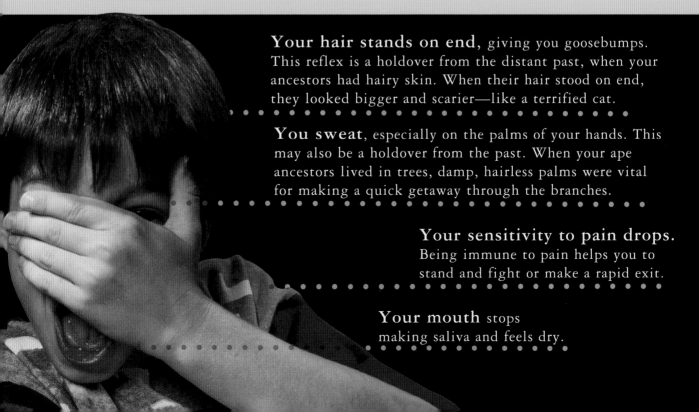

Your hair stands on end, giving you goosebumps. This reflex is a holdover from the distant past, when your ancestors had hairy skin. When their hair stood on end, they looked bigger and scarier—like a terrified cat.

You sweat, especially on the palms of your hands. This may also be a holdover from the past. When your ape ancestors lived in trees, damp, hairless palms were vital for making a quick getaway through the branches.

Your sensitivity to pain drops. Being immune to pain helps you to stand and fight or make a rapid exit.

Your mouth stops making saliva and feels dry.

A phobia is like a *car alarm* going off by accident

Do you have a

What is phobia?

Someone who has a **specific phobia** suffers from a full-blown feeling of terror when they see a certain trigger, such as a snake or a spider. Before they have time to think, the **limbic system** in the brain has put the body on red alert and caused all the symptoms of fear, including a racing heart, a queasy stomach, and a feeling of utter **dread**.

Why snakes and spiders?

People have an inborn tendency to develop phobias of **animals**. Psychologists think this is because poisonous or aggressive animals were serious dangers in our distant, evolutionary past, and we still carry the genes that can trigger fear of them.

Why are phobias irrational?

Fear happens below the level of conscious thought, and this is why phobias can be triggered by things we know are not really dangerous. It is possible to suppress the feeling of fear with thought, but the initial **gut reaction** is hard to prevent.

phobia?

What gives people phobias?

According to some surveys, as many as one in ten people have a phobia. Identical twins often have the same phobia, which suggests that genes play a role in causing phobias. But most phobias are probably learned. As children, we learn what to fear by **watching other people**. If we see someone reacting in terror to something, we are quite likely to become afraid of it ourselves.

Do you have...

... a fear of spiders, blood, or heights? Most true phobias involve animals, disease, or dangerous situations:

 gephyrophobia
fear of crossing bridges

 aerophobia
fear of flying

 musophobia
fear of rats

 myrmecophobia
fear of ants

 batrachophobia
fear of frogs, toads, and newts

 vertigo
fear of heights

 amaxophobia
fear of vehicles

 alektorophobia
fear of chickens

 arachnophobia
fear of spiders

 ichthyophobia
fear of fish

 ailurophobia
fear of cats

 hemophobia
fear of blood

Some "phobias" are really just dislikes. The phobias below don't cause genuine fear:

 pogonophobia
fear of beards

 xanthophobia
fear of yellow

 chronometrophobia
fear of clocks

 blennophobia
fear of slime

 scopophobia
fear of being stared at

8 **octophobia**
fear of the number 8

 panophobia
fear of everything

 arachibutyrophobia
fear of peanut butter sticking to the roof of the mouth

 iophobia
fear of poisons and rust

 didaskaleinophobia
fear of going to school

 pteronophobia
fear of being tickled by feathers

 geniophobia
fear of chins

HOW TO SPOT A LIAR

People don't just lie with their voice—they also use phony expressions and gestures. But there are a few giveaway clues:

Blushing

Some people blush involuntarily when they're lying or embarrassed about being caught out.

Microexpressions

Skilled liars can look convincingly happy or sad, but if you watch carefully, you might see true expressions appear fleetingly—for less than a fifth of a second.

Suppressed expressions

Less skilled liars can sometimes be seen trying to **suppress** facial expressions—they might try to hide a smirk, for example.

Honest muscles

Some muscles in the face are more honest than others, especially those around the **eyebrows**. A liar might be smiling, for instance, but an eyebrow might rise or twitch because they feel uncomfortable.

Touching the face

Small children often cover their mouths when lying. Adults and older children use similar but more subtle gestures, like touching the nose or scratching a lip.

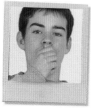

Can you read FACES?

Head movements are usually easy to interpret. A slightly tilted head can be a sign of **interest**, while a head resting on a hand suggests boredom. Turning the head away can be a sign of rejection, but it is also a sign of concentration. If someone tilts back their head slightly, it might mean they think they're **superior**.

Eyes give away a lot. If you follow someone's gaze, you'll often see what they're thinking about. When someone is excited, their pupils **dilate**, and this is impossible to fake. Exposing the whites of the eyes above the iris is a sign of fear or shock. Rolling back the eyes to show the lower white is a sign of **contempt**, often done secretly behind someone's back.

Normal pupil   *Dilated pupil*   *White of eye exposed*   *Rolling the eyes*

Mouth movements play a role in many obvious expressions, including frowns and smiles, but they can also give away hidden feelings. Tightly closed lips show **suppressed anger**, for instance, and a yawn may be a sign of fear or nerves rather than tiredness. Sucking a pen or biting a fingernail can be signs of tension, and lopsided smiles show lack of interest.

Smile   *Thin lips*   *Yawn*   *Nail-biting*

Psychologists think we have about 7,000 different facial expressions, and these can flit across our faces with amazing speed, often without our realizing it. To a large extent, your social skills depend on how good you are at reading people's faces and decoding their inner thoughts and feelings—especially when they are hiding something or being dishonest.

Eye contact is the key to good communication,
but how much is the right amount? Prolonged eye contact can be a sign of aggression or **attraction**; very little eye contact may mean dishonesty, shyness, or dislike. In most conversations, eye contact is a matter of give and take, with frequent breaks. When people are **flirting**, eye contact lasts longer and the eyes rove down the face.

Eyebrows are among the most honest parts of the face.
Watch the skin above and between them—when someone is worried or uneasy, small wrinkles appear without their realizing.

Eyelids show several emotions. Rapid blinking indicates tension
or fascination, but blinking may stop altogether if someone is lying or angry. A spasm of **eyelid fluttering** is a sure sign of nerves.

Raised eyebrow

Furrowed brow

Blinking

Nose movements usually show negative emotions.
When the nose and brow wrinkle up severely, a person is disgusted. A faint wrinkling merely shows dislike, and a twitch to the side might show disagreement. If a person's nostrils flare open, they may find you attractive.

Twitch to side

Slightly wrinkled

Very wrinkled

Flared nostrils

HOW TO SPOT A FAKE SMILE

The trick to spotting a fake smile is to look at the smiler's eyes.

- A real smile spreads across the **whole face**, raising the cheeks and making the eyes wrinkle up.

- Crow's feet form beside the eyes, bags appear under them, and the eyebrows are lowered. In a fake smile, the mouth moves but the eyes stay **cold and neutral**.

- Fake smiles tend to be somewhat mistimed. They can appear too quickly and **end abruptly**. They may also last too long (a frozen smile) or be too short (on–off smile).

- Real smiles are usually very **symmetrical**, but fake smiles can look **crooked** and painful.

CAN *YOU* SPOT ANY FAKES?

1

2

3

4

5

6

See page 96 for the answers.

What's your BODY LANGUAGE?

People enter our **social zone** in public places, such as stores or sidewalks.

The **personal zone** is used for polite conversation.

Personal space

How close to us we allow other people to come depends on how well we know them. Strangers usually get no closer than the social or personal zone, and only best friends and family can enter the intimate zones. The limits of your zones depends on your personality and the culture you grow up in.

Heads facing but bodies turned away can be a sign of conflict.

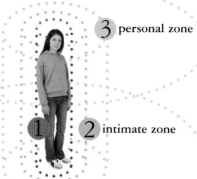

4 social zone

3 personal zone

1

2 intimate zone

close intimate zone

The **close intimate zone** is for physical contact.

Words and facial expressions aren't the only way we **communicate**—we also use our bodies. Some of our gestures are deliberate, but a lot of our body language is **unconscious**. We also read body language

This boy has a relaxed and **open** posture—a sign of confidence or perhaps arrogance.

Politicians sometimes use the **power grip** during a speech.

Hiding the hands and looking down both show submissiveness.

These girls are unconsciously copying each other.

DOMINANCE

Someone who feels superior or **powerful** shows it with a relaxed posture. Relaxing is normal when with friends and family, but in the company of strangers, it can appear cocky.

SUBMISSION

Submissive is the opposite of powerful. A submissive person stands still or sits upright, with their hands held down.

MIMICKING

When two people get along very well, they often **mimic** each other's body language without realizing it.

By keeping their bodies facing each other, these two people are **excluding** the third person.

As well as turning toward each other, these girls are pointing with their feet. The boy feels shut out.

This girl secretly likes the boy with red hair.

Aggression

When a fight is brewing between boys, they will **square off**, with faces facing but bodies turned away a little. Their eyes glower and they stop blinking.

POINTING WITH THE BODY

In a social situation like a party, the direction your body faces is important. Two people can make a third person feel **unwelcome** by keeping their bodies turned toward each other. Even if they occasionally turn their heads to be polite, the third person will feel excluded and awkward. People may unwittingly point with a part of the body toward someone or something they are secretly thinking about.

unconsciously—you might get a feeling that someone likes or dislikes you without knowing why. Body language sends **powerful signals**, and it can give away your secret feelings.

Rubbing an eye

Fidgeting hand and foot

Pulling an ear

Crossed ankles and clenched hands

Folded arms and legs

DISHONESTY

People usually feel uncomfortable when they lie, and this can make them **fidget** or touch themselves. As well as touching their faces, liars might shift in their chairs or start moving a foot restlessly.

DEFENSIVENESS

When people feel anxious or defensive, they unconsciously adopt **closed** postures. Crossed ankles can mean someone is hiding negative feelings. The **foot lock** (center) is a typically female gesture that reveals a defensive attitude.

FAQ

How did I learn to speak?

Babies have an **instinctive** ability to pick up language without being taught. They listen intently to voices, even before they are born. At birth they can babble in all the vowels and consonants of all the world's languages,  but by 6 months this has narrowed down to the language they hear. By age 3 they've picked up most of the important words in this language.

Where does my accent come from?

The language you speak and your accent depend on **where you live**. Most people pick up their accent (as well as slang words) from their friends rather than their parents, so the way you speak might be quite different from your parents. In childhood, you can pick up any accent and learn any language fluently, but by about the age of 11 the circuits in your brain that pick up new sounds wither away. As a result, the accent you have in your teens will probably stick with you for life.

How big is my vocabulary?

The words you know depend on your age, how much you read, and the language you speak. The average American high-school student knows about **40,000 words**, which is barely a tenth of the total number of words in the English language. Even so, it's more than enough —most people use only one or two thousand words in everyday life.

Do you have a way with WORDS?

Your genes build the basic apparatus you need for speech, but almost everything about the way you speak depends on your upbringing, from your **accent** and **language** to your choice of **words**—and even your sense of humor!

Where does my voice come from?

Your voice comes from your **vocal cords**—two vibrating cords of tissue in your voice box, deep in your throat. **Touch your throat** while you speak to feel your vocal cords vibrate. Try the same thing when whispering and you won't feel a thing because you're only using your mouth to make sound. Your mouth is vital to all speech. It shapes sound to make vowels— look in a mirror as you say **ooo, eee, aaa**. You also use your lips, tongue, and teeth for consonants. Try reading this sentence out loud without closing your lips to see why.

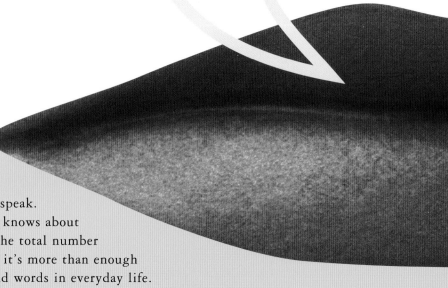

Yikes, a leopard!

CAN ANIMALS TALK?
Animals communicate in lots of ways —by growling, singing, squeaking, scent-marking, and using all sorts of body language. Some animals, such as meerkats, even have a small **vocabulary** of calls to warn each other of different predators, such as eagles, leopards, and snakes.

But there's one thing that humans alone are capable of: grammar. Using the rules of grammar, we can arrange words in different combinations to create sentences, each with a unique meaning that can be clearly understood.

The only voice you never hear properly is *your own*

What does my voice sound like?
You hear your own voice partly as vibrations in your skull, so you never hear it properly. Record it and play it back to see what it really sounds like. The basic sound and pitch of your voice depend on the size and shape of your voice box and mouth. But the vowels and consonants you can say depend on your language and culture.

FAQ

What are gestures for?
To see how important hand gestures are to speech, try describing a spiral in words alone, or try keeping your hands still next time you're on the phone. We pick up gestures by unconsciously **copying** the people around us as we grow up. The way you walk, stand, sit, and move your hands all probably come from copying your family.

What makes you laugh?
According to studies of identical twins, your sense of humor— like your accent and language— comes from the environment you grow up in and not from your genes. Laughter is a vital part of the way we communicate because it strengthens social bonds. Some scientists think it has the same physical effect as **grooming** does in monkeys. Monkeys spend hours every day grooming the fur of relatives and best friends. Doing so triggers the release of brain chemicals called **endorphins**, which relieve tension.

What's dyslexia?
Some people find learning to read and write unusually difficult because of a problem known as **dyslexia**. A dyslexic person might find it very difficult to tell the difference between the letters "b" and "d" or the numbers "6" and "9," for instance. Dyslexic people are just as intelligent as other people and often go on to be very successful in life.

What's my POTENTIAL?

Play to your STRENGTHS

Achieving your potential is all about knowing what you're good at and playing to your strengths. Psychologists recognize at least seven different areas of natural ability, or "intelligence." What **skills** do you have?

- **Interpersonal** Are you quick to see what other people are thinking or feeling?
- **Intrapersonal** Do you truly understand your own feelings and emotions—do you have "self-knowledge"?
- **Physical** Are you quick to master physical skills like driving, skiing, sports, or new dance steps?
- **Musical** Can you hum a song after hearing it once, and can you sing in perfect tune?
- **Spatial** Do you find reading maps and tinkering with machines easy?
- **Verbal** Are you an avid reader or good at writing?
- **Logical** Do you find things like math and computers easy to understand?

What about my WEAKNESSES?

Being bad at something often doesn't matter. If you can't draw, it's unlikely to stop you from becoming a CEO or an Olympic athlete. There are some areas of ability, however, that are important for everyone and worth trying to improve. All of us come in contact with other people at home and at work or school, which makes interpersonal skills very important. People with good interpersonal skills have a **head start** in life and often rise quickly through the ranks in their profession. People with less ability may struggle to succeed unless they learn to behave in a more socially skilled way. And these skills can certainly be learned—and are indeed learned by almost everyone as they grow up.

Can I be a SUCCESS?

You need only two things to be a success: a certain amount of natural ability, and the willingness to **persevere**. Even geniuses need to work very hard to succeed. As the inventor Thomas Edison said, "genius is one percent inspiration and 99 percent perspiration." The composer Mozart was a musical genius, but only after years of training. In fact, he had already spent 5 years performing by the age of 12. Likewise, Albert Einstein spent his childhood reading very difficult books on mathematics and philosophy. Real top-quality genius isn't just about hard work, though—it also requires **creative thinking** and leaps of imagination. A genius breaks the mold and discovers new ways of doing things that everybody else copies. So what's the secret of creativity? Psychologists figure it takes about **10,000 hours** of practice at something to become so good that you are truly creative. It sounds like a lot, but it's only 5 years!

What is the secret of HAPPINESS?

What's the point of being successful if it doesn't make you happy? For most people, the ultimate ambition in life is to be **happy**. People have been searching for the secret of happiness for thousands of years, and recently psychologists have joined the hunt. If their research is right, the secret of happiness is actually very simple. First of all, it helps if you enjoy meeting people and don't spend too much time alone. Second, you're more likely to be happy if your expectations aren't too high. And third, don't forget to look on the bright side of things!

The secret of *success* is to know what

you're good at and play to your STRENGTHS

GLOSSARY

Adolescence the period of life between childhood and adulthood.

Adrenaline the "fight or flight" hormone, which prepares the body for rapid action.

Allergen a harmless protein (or protein-carbohydrate complex) that can trigger the immune system, causing an allergy. Pollen is a common allergen.

Allergy abnormal reaction of the immune system to a harmless substance, such as pollen or dust.

Amygdala an almond-shaped structure in the limbic system of the brain. It plays an important role in emotion.

Antibody a protein made by certain types of white blood cells. Each type of antibody has a specific shape that enables it to bind to specific germs.

Artery a thick-walled blood vessel containing blood flowing away from the heart.

Atom a tiny particle of matter that cannot be divided (except in a nuclear explosion).

Bacteria microscopic, single-celled organisms that are common in all living or dead organic matter. Some bacteria cause disease.

Capillary one of the microscopic blood vessels through which blood reaches all the body's cells.

Carbon one of the main elements in the human body. Carbon atoms link together to form long chains in organic molecules.

Cell one of the microscopic building blocks that make up living organisms. Cells normally have a jellylike filling and an outer membrane.

Cerebellum a cauliflower-shaped structure at the back of the brain that plays an important role in balance and coordinating muscle movements.

Cerebral cortex the wrinkly outer part of the brain.

Chromosome one of a set of microscopic structures inside cells that carry DNA.

Clone an organism that has been grown from a body cell of another organism and is genetically identical to it. Identical twins are natural clones.

Conscious awake and aware of the world.

DNA deoxyribonucleic acid, a very long, helical molecule that carries genes as a chemical code.

DNA fingerprint a pattern of stripes obtained by breaking down someone's DNA and separating the fragments in gel. Police and forensic scientists use DNA fingerprints to identify people.

Dominant a gene that overpowers another gene is said to be dominant. Dominant can also refer to a person who acts in a bossy or overpowering way.

Egg cell a female sex cell.

Element a chemical that cannot be broken down into simpler chemicals.

Embryo the earliest stage of development in a plant or animal.

Endorphin a kind of neurotransmitter that relieves pain when it is released in the brain.

Enzyme a protein that speeds up the rate of a particular chemical reaction. Digestive enzymes speed up chemical reactions that break down large organic molecules into smaller fragments.

Fertilization the fusion of a sperm cell and egg cell to create a new individual.

Frontal lobes two main divisions of the cerebral cortex. The frontal lobes are important in planning and making decisions.

Gene an instruction carried by the DNA molecule. Genes are passed from parents to offspring during reproduction.

Genome the full set of genes in an organism.

Germ any microscopic organism that can cause disease, such as a bacterium or virus.

Hemoglobin the oxygen-carrying protein in red blood cells. Hemoglobin contains iron and gives blood its color.

Hippocampus a seahorse-shaped structure in the brain that plays a role in laying down memories.

Histamine a chemical released by white blood cells that makes tissue become tender and inflamed. Histamine is released during allergic reactions or when germs or dirt enter the body.

Hormone a substance that is released into the blood by a gland and has far-reaching effects on other parts of the body.

Immune system a complex system of tissues and cells that defend the body against invading germs, such as bacteria and viruses.

IQ intelligence quotient, a measure of intelligence derived from a test of numerical, spatial, and verbal abilities.

Iris the colored part of the eye. The iris is a muscle that controls the size of the pupil.

Joint the meeting point between two bones.

Limbic system a collection of structures in the center of the brain that play an important role in emotion and subconscious processes.

Molecule a group of chemically combined atoms. A water molecule, for example, is made of two hydrogen atoms and one oxygen atom (H_2O).

Mucus a thick, sticky fluid produced by the inner lining of the mouth, nose, throat, and intestines.

Nerve a bundle of long nerve-cell fibers. Nerves carry electrical signals between the brain and the body.

Neuron a nerve cell or brain cell.

Neurotransmitter a chemical that crosses the microscopic gap (synapse) between two neurons, passing a signal from one neuron to the next.

Organ a large body structure with a specific function, such as the heart, stomach, or brain.

Organ transplant an operation in which a surgeon replaces a diseased organ with a healthy organ taken from another person.

Oxygen the gas that blood absorbs from the air when we breathe. Our cells need oxygen to release energy from food.

Placenta the organ through which a developing baby absorbs oxygen and nutrients from its mother while it is still in the womb. The baby is linked to the placenta by an umbilical cord.

Protein a complex biological molecule made of a chain of units called amino acids. Muscle and hair are mostly protein. Protein molecules called enzymes control most of the chemical reactions in living organisms.

Psychoanalyst someone who attempts to treat a patient by discussing their dreams, memories, and childhood family relationships. Sigmund Freud was the father of psychoanalysis.

Psychologist a scientist who studies the mind, behavior, and personality of people.

Puberty the stage of development when the body becomes capable of sexual reproduction.

Pupil The black circle in the middle of the eye. The pupil is a hole that lets light enter the eye.

Recessive gene a gene that is overpowered by a dominant gene.

Sensory cortex the part of the brain that processes information coming in from the senses.

Sperm male sex cells, made by the testis.

Subconscious below the level of consciousness. Subconscious processes happen in the brain without your being aware of them.

Sympathetic nervous system one of the two main divisions of the involuntary part of the body's nervous system. The sympathetic nervous system prepares the body for action.

Tendon a very tough fibrous connection that ties a muscle to a bone.

Testosterone the male sex hormone. Testosterone triggers the development of male characteristics at puberty.

Tissue an assemblage of cells of a similar type, such as skin, bone, or muscle.

Vein a thin-walled blood vessel containing blood flowing back to the heart.

Virus a very simple type of organism consisting of a length of DNA, usually in a protein coat. Viruses reproduce by infecting cells, often causing disease.

Vitamin a complex organic compound needed by the body in very small quantities.

INDEX

ACKNOWLEDGMENTS

Dorling Kindersley would like to thank the following people for help with this book: Janet Allis, Penny Arlon, Maree Carroll, Andy Crawford, Tory Gordon-Harris, Lorrie Mack, Pilar Morales for digital artwork, Laura Roberts, Cheryl Telfer, Martin Wilson.

Thanks also to Somso Modelle for use of their anatomical model (p. 16)
The publisher would like to thank the following for their kind permission to reproduce their images: Position key: a=above, b=below/bottom, c=centre, l=left, r=right, t=top

Corbis: Bettmann 77cl; Cameron 57tr; Cheque 36-37b; L. Clarke 37tr; Robert Holmes 52cb; Richard Hutchings 22crb; Thom Lang 6tl, 13bcr, 14clb (brain); Lawrence Manning 35bl; John-Marshall Mantel 52ca; Reuters 28bc; Anthony Redpath 1tl (photos); ROB & SAS 33br; Royalty Free Images 29tc (mouth), 79c; Nancy A. Santullo 64bc, 70tl; Norbert Schaefer 36-37c; Strauss/Curtis 22l, 78r; Mark Tuschman 64clb, 78l; Larry Williams 34c; Elizabeth Young 34cl. DK Images: Commisioner for the City of London Police 73cr; Denoyer/Geppert Intl. 17clb, 19tr, 20tr; Eddie Lawrence 59tr; Judith Miller, Otford Antiques & Collectors Centre, Kent 64cb (bear), 67bl, 69clb; 16r Jerry Young

Berg 26-27; Tipp Howell 49cra; Andreas Kuehn 64ca (face), 79r; Stuart McClymont 52c; Eric O'Connell 80-81b; Royalty Free/Alan Bailey 64br, 78c; Chip Simons 77r; Anna Summa 79l, 85bcl; Trujillo-Paumier 64tr, 76-77b; V.C.L. 36cl; David Zelick 34tr. Science Photo Library: 10l, 11tl, 11tr, 11l, 11r, 14crb (left jar), 14crb (right jar), 15cl, 18cl; Alex Bartel 39cr; Annabella Bluesky 22cra, 35br; Neil Bromhall 39cl; BSIP Ducloux 22cr; BSIP, Joubert 18cla; BSIP/Serconi 11tcl; BSIP VEM 18clb, 78bl; Scott Camazine 19bl; CNRI 6cr, 13bcl, 17clb, 20cla, 20bl; Dept. of Clinical Cytogenetics, Addenbrookes Hospital 33bc; John Dougherty 12bl; Eye of Science 19clb, 20cl; David Gifford 6, 22tr; Pascal Goetcheluck 28tcr; Nancy Kedersha 5cl, 44-45; Mehau Kulyk 11tc, 18r, 30clb; Francis Leroy, Biocosmos 38l; Dick Luria 21bl; David M. Martin, M.D. 19cl; Hank Morgan 29bc, 29tc (graphic), 47br, 81tr; Dr. G. Moscoso 38r; Prof. P. Motta, Dept. of Anatomy, University "La Sapienza", Rome 15cla; Profs. P.M. Motta & S. Makabe 38cr; Dr. Yorgos Nikas 38cl; David Parker 28tcl; Alfred Pasieka 29bl, 46-47c(brain); Prof. Aaron Polliack 10r, 14crb (middle jar); Victor De Schwanberg 12bcl, 13tr, 14clb (heart), 14clb (kidney); Volker Steger 58tl, 72-73; VVG 6tr, 21crb; Andrew Syred 6clb, 11tcr, 17cla, 21cl, 28tr, 30cl; Paul Taylor 12bcr; Tissuepix 39l; Geoff Tompkinson 46bl; 83 (car) National Motor Museum, Beaulieu, Somso Modelle 14tl.

ANSWERS

Page 51
LEFT OR RIGHT

You will almost certainly have gotten farther through the dots with one hand. This is your dominant hand and the one you use for writing. If you got equally far with both hands, consider yourself extremely unusual— almost everybody has a preference for one hand or the other.

Page 54
HOW'S YOUR MEMORY FOR WORDS?

If you scored more than 8, well done. Words are harder to remember than faces, but easier than numbers. You probably found unusual words (like "vomit") easier to remember than boring ones (like "salad"). That's because your brain is good at paying attention to anything unusual. You may have found that your visual memory helped on this test, especially if you joined words in odd combinations, like jam on a carpet or a pebble on a chair.

Page 55
HOW'S YOUR VISUAL MEMORY?

If you remembered more than half of the objects, well done. This test is harder than the word test because you can't use your imagination to create memorable images. The objects on the tray are uninteresting and unlikely to stay long in your short-term memory.

Page 55
NUMBER CRUNCHER

Most people can keep only 7 digits at a time in their short-term memory, so if you got more than this, well done. Numbers are much harder to remember than words or pictures because they are much less interesting. However, you can improve your memory of a long number by saying it so many times that your brain remembers the sound of the words. This works even if you say the words silently in your head without speaking them. If something distracts you while you're doing this, the number will quickly disappear from your short-term memory.

Pages 60-61
SPATIAL INTELLIGENCE

1e, 2b, 3b, 4e, 5d, 6a, 7d, 8b, 9b, 10e

Pages 60-61
VERBAL INTELLIGENCE

1c, 2d, 3a, 4d, 5e, 6c, 7e, 8d, 9a, 10c, 11d, 12c, 13e, 14a, 15b, 16b

Pages 62-63
NUMERICAL INTELLIGENCE

1e, 2e, 3a, 4d (each pair of numbers adds up to the next one in the sequence), 5b, 6a (the numbers show the position of each letter in the alphabet), 7e, 8d (be careful—it's a trick question!), 9d, 10c (another trick question!), 11d, 12a, 13b, 14b (all the numbers are squares), 15c

Pages 62-63
LATERAL INTELLIGENCE

1. A chick inside an egg.
2. They were part of a snowman's face in winter, but the snowman melted.
3. The backpack contains his parachute, which failed to open.
4. They are triplets.
5. A square utility cover can fall down the hole if you turn it, but a round one can't.
6. The punch contained ice cubes made from poisonous water. The ice melted after the man left.
7. Nothing.
8. Turn the first switch on and leave the second switch off. Turn the third switch on for two minutes and then turn it off. Run upstairs—one of the lights (switch 1) will be on and one of the other light bulbs (switch 3) will be warm. The cold light bulb is switch 2.
9. The man is a dwarf and can't reach higher than button 7 in the elevator. On rainy days he carries an umbrella and can use it to push the top button.

Page 75
OWL OR LARK

Score 4 points for each A, 3 points for each B, 2 points for each C, 1 point for each D.

6–11 points. You're an owl and you love staying up late. But you might be sleep-deprived, which could make you bad-tempered during the day and affect your schoolwork. Try going to bed a little earlier on weekdays if you think you need more sleep.

12–18 points. You're neither an owl nor a lark, and you probably have sensible sleep habits.

19–24 points. You're a lark and you love the mornings. Consider yourself lucky—most people hate getting up early.

Page 85
SPOT THE FAKE SMILE

1, 2, and 3 are fake; 4, 5, and 6 are real.